let them Play

The Importance of Play and 100 Child Development Activities

Dr. Magdalena Battles

Thank you, God, for my children, for without them there would be no reason for me to play like I do every day. My family gives me reason to play and live joyfully.

I am grateful to God for the blessing of my family.

Dedicated To:

My wonderful husband Justin.
I wouldn't want to go through life and raise our family
with anyone else in the world. I love you.

And

Our children Brielle, Alexander, & Charles (and our angel Barron)
who are my reason for playing and finding joy daily.

THANK YOU

A very special thank you to Jessy Kuruvilla who is the founder, director, and head teacher at I Can Academy in Southlake, TX. Thank you for allowing our family to be a part of your school. It was the best year of my twin's lives so far! The year at your school was filled with joy, play, learning, the best field trips, and wonderful experiences for our family. We are thankful for your love, teaching methods, and passion for your school families. I wish every child could experience a preschool like yours, for our world would be forever changed for the better! We love you Miss Jessy!

Thank you to the families of I Can Academy for allowing our family to be a part of your lives for the past year. You have each imprinted on our hearts for a lifetime. Thank you also for granting permission for photos of your children to be used in this book. I pray that other children can learn, play, and benefit developmentally from the photos of your children and the activities they are doing in this book.

Thank you to Leon Ho, who is the founder and CEO of www.LifeHack.com, my LifeHack editor Anna Chui, and to the staff at LifeHack for the opportunity to write and share my expertise on your website. It is a pleasure working with you all! I am proud to be a part of the LifeHack team.

Thank you to Melinda Martin, Shayla Raquel, Lori Walker, and Mike Jacquart for your expertise and service. You made this book possible.

Thank you to my best friend Rachel Pierce. You are the best supporter, encourager, friend, and sister anyone could ever dream to have. I am lucky to have you in my life. I love you so much!

CONTENTS

Part I: The Importance of Play

Part II: 100+ Child Development Play Activities

A Word of Caution

Please use caution when using the activities in this book with your children. Be aware that although the activities in this book are intended for children ages 2–8 it does not mean that each activity is safe or should be used with all ages. Some activities are intended for younger children, while others are better suited for older children. When deciding which activities to utilize with your children, the most important factor is safety. Read the safety warnings on all toys. There are many activities in this book that are not suited for children who place objects in their mouths. Do not give children small objects if they tend to put small things in their mouths. Do not give sharp objects to small children. Use your best judgment and when in doubt, do not allow the child to participate in an activity or play with a toy if you are unsure whether it is safe. All the activities in this book are intended to be done under adult supervision. If you choose to engage in the activities published in this book you do so at your own risk. The author and publisher disclaim all responsibility for any injury or damage caused by engaging in any of the activities in this book. Please use your best judgment, discernment, and caution when implementing any play activity with children.

PART I

The Importance of Play

We recently installed a waterslide in our pool. It has led to hours and hours of fun—literally days of fun when you count all the hours my three kids have spent on it in the past month. They climb the nine stairs and then steady themselves on top of the eight-foot slide with water rushing under their feet as they move to a sitting or lying position. They push off in order to plunge down; while making swooshing sounds, the slide takes them on a slight twist to the right. Finally, they free fall into the pool with a big splash making squeals of joy and delight. They will go on this slide repeatedly for hours. We can spend an entire afternoon in the pool with them going down continually until it is time to go inside for dinner.

Would you believe it if I told you that while they are going down the slide, they are getting developmental benefits that help with their ability to learn? It is true. They are learning and developing because of this simple activity of playing on a slide. Slide play helps children with their gross motor skill development. It also engages and stimulates their senses. Playing on a slide helps children improve their balance, coordination, and muscle tone. It is good for their body and their mind, as it engages both simultaneously.

Slide play is also beneficial to vestibular development. Our vestibular system contributes to hand-eye coordination, posture control, spatial orientation, and can be regarded as a spatial orientation system (Cohen and Keshner, 1989). Active playground movements that affect the inner ear and balance, such as spinning, sliding, rocking, and jumping help children with their vestibular development (Integrated Learning Strategies, 2016).

This means that because play is more than meets the eye, vestibular development occurs while my children are playing on our waterslide. Play is life changing for children, because it is how they learn and develop. Children who are not exposed to play, such as that of physical playground activities, do not reap the developmental benefits from this kind of play, and consequently may suffer from developmental deficits such as low vestibular development (Integrated Learning Strategies, 2016).

Our slide, and how it benefits my children developmentally, is just one example of the developmental advantages that play provides. It wasn't purchased purely to entertain them in the pool for hours during our summer break from school, but that may have had a lot to do with it. However, we know it is much more than just mindless fun. There are serious developmental benefits to playground activities like sliding, swinging, and climbing.

This is good news for us as parents. It means we don't have to work so hard! We can let them play! Play is beneficial to children in so many ways, probably even more ways than researchers have uncovered thus far.

Why Play Matters

Researchers are learning more about play and its benefits for children every year. We are learning things about play that challenge traditional classroom learning methods being utilized with preschool-aged children. Sitting still and silent at a desk with a pencil and paper in hand, repeatedly writing the same letters or words are no longer believed to be the best way for children to learn. The National Association for the Education of Young Children (NAEYC, 2009), a highly regarded professional organization for early childhood education professionals, emphasizes the importance of play with children as a central component to their learning and development. The NAEYC (2009, p. 14) stated the following about play in their position statement:

> *"Play is an important vehicle for developing self-regulation as well as for promoting language, cognition, and social competence."*

Bongiorno (2018) explains how there is a shift in many parents' thinking when their children go from toddler to preschool age. Parents are in favor of play when their children are toddlers, just learning to walk and talk. Their playtime is cute and appropriate. However, when the child becomes a preschooler and is ready to begin preparing for school, many parents believe that their child should be sitting at a desk in a preschool classroom completing workbooks. Bongiorno explains that this is simply not the best method for learning at that age. Young children learn best through play methods. These methods can be targeted for the development of specific skills including cognitive, social, emotional, language, physical, and more.

Play is to be nurtured, so that children can learn and prepare for school gradually. Directed play that enhances specific skills such as fine motor development, social skills, and hand-eye coordination is beneficial to children as they get ready for more formal learning. Play and development go hand-in-hand. Through play children develop in all areas: cognitively, physically, emotionally, and socially. Play is a child's way of exploring the world. It also allows them to use creative thought processes and explore their imagination. When their play is limited, their creativity is also limited.

An Example of Why Play Matters

When children participate in pretend play and role play, they are learning about the real world. It is their way of practicing for life in the real world. For example, they may watch you make dinner for the family. They observe you using the stove, stirring the pot of spaghetti as it cooks. They see you touch the pan accidently and you say "ouch, that's hot." Later that evening you watch your child as they actively play in their own play kitchen. They pull out some plastic pots and pans, then add some plastic and wooden food play items to these pots. They stir just like they observed you stirring. Then they touch the play stove, and yell "ouch, I burned myself, the stove is hot!" They learn through watching and they then act out their observations. You may not always see it clearly, but your children are learning through the emulation of your activities and others that they watch throughout the course of their day.

Playtime gives children the opportunity to practice these skills themselves and experience what it would feel like to do what they saw you doing. For example, cooking in the kitchen, putting food in pots, stirring, setting the table for eating, and serving others are all done in playtime because they witnessed you doing these actions. They role and pretend play these same activities as practice for real life. It is crucial to their development. Play is their way to experiment with real life activities in a safe and fun way.

The World Economic Forum's Assessment of Play

The World Economic Forum has featured many articles on the topic of play. This forum has produced research and writings that greatly support the need for play in early childhood. John Goodwin, CEO of the LEGO Foundation, gave an important presentation on play at the 2018 World Economic Forum. Here is what he had to say at the annual meeting about the importance and value of play:

> *"Real play is the freedom for children to engage with and learn from the world that surrounds them. By mentally and physically connecting children to the world, play empowers them to create and grow for the rest of their lives. It is a fundamental right for all children.*
>
> *Research shows that play is vital to a child's development, equipping them with the skills necessary to tackle humanity's future, such as emotional intelligence, creativity and problem solving. To be a superhero is to lead; to host a teddy for tea is to organize; to build a fort is to innovate; to play is to learn."*

The importance of play for our children should not be undermined by educational ambitions. We want our children to succeed so badly that we are pushing them too early into classroom-style learning, which involves sitting at desks, and listening to instructional lessons. When this happens, we are limiting their opportunities for creativity to blossom through imaginative play. If a teacher tells them how to play with a toy, they learn how to use the toy according to the teacher's instruction. If we hand the toy to a child and tell them to figure it out themselves, they will likely not only figure it out, but also find additional creative ways for playing with the toy. However, they need the freedom of time and space to explore through play for these problem-solving skills and creative thought processes to be maximized.

Goodwin (2018) went on to state the following about play and the future of our children:

> *"The more our children play today, the more prepared future generations will be. Play is needed to endow us with leaders who can resolve conflict, problem solve, build socially connected communities and inspire society to flourish. We are committed to the idea that any child, wherever they are in the world, could be such a leader. Join us in protecting their real play."*

Play is crucial to ensuring our children develop unique abilities to become creative problem solvers who can change the world with their leadership. We must protect our children's right to play. Providing them the opportunities to play both at home and in the classroom is critical.

Overstressing Our Kids—and the Solution

Kids are increasingly overstressed because they are over-schooled, overscheduled, and pressured to perform academically. Our society is increasingly competitive when it comes to children's schooling and producing high scores on standardized tests. Since when have we decided as a society that school test scores or IQ scores are the greatest predictor of our children's success? I don't know who made that decision, but I am not in agreement with it. Tests do not predict a child's ability to succeed in the world. Harvard researcher Angela Duckworth (2016) is the author of the book *Grit*. She found that grit is a better predictor of success than IQ scores. This means we can ease up on the standardized tests, because we are only proving that kids are good at taking tests, not that they are competent in real life skills.

Play is what builds real life skills. The importance of play cannot be stressed enough in our world today. Creativity is dying in our culture because of the overworked and overscheduled nature of our lives and the lives of our children. The way to increase creativity is to allow more time for children to play. Free play is crucial to the development of creativity.

In my popular LifeHack.org article titled "The Endless Battle Between School Work and Play for Children", I addressed this issue of our children not being allowed enough time to play and the repercussions of overscheduling.

> *"Parents who are pushing their kids toward success are unfortunately harming their kid's creativity. It happens when there isn't enough time in the day to allow kids to simply play. Many adults are continually overscheduling children and keeping the lives of these kids so structured that free play is an afterthought. But the need for play to ignite creativity in children is real. Children need time to play freely and this allows their creativity to flourish.*
>
> *Imaginative play becomes scarce when children aren't given the opportunity and are instead in the classroom all day long beginning at toddler ages. The consequence of this loss of creativity is a society of educated people who lack creativity.*
>
> *A study by Live Science discussed research on this subject and stated, [2]*

"Since 1990, children have become less able to produce unique and unusual ideas. They are also less humorous, less imaginative and less able to elaborate on ideas."

Also contributing to a decrease in childhood creativity is, the way mainstream education forces kids to suppress their creativity because what is rewarded is standardized test scores. This is not all schools, but this is the current trend in our mainstream education systems. The World Economic Forum discusses the problem of creativity being suppressed in the classroom and stated the following,

"Worryingly, these skills are often not featured prominently in children's school day where the norm still is the chalk-and-talk teaching approach that has prevailed for centuries.""

The time has come when we each need to personally assess our family's level of busyness, as well as our personal level of activities. If our family and children are kept so busy that free play time is minimal each day, then we may want to seriously consider changing some things in our lives. Our children only get to experience childhood once, so let's not rush them to adulthood and skip out on the opportunity for them to learn, grow, and develop through meaningful play.

Teaching Them to Read Early May Not Give Them an Academic Edge

There is increasing pressure on children to read at younger and younger ages. When I was a child we didn't begin to learn to read until first grade. Kindergarten was filled with play centers, singing the alphabet, and counting to one hundred. However, this is no longer the case. Many schools in the United States now make it standard practice to teach children to read in kindergarten. This was true for my daughter. It was a stressful year for all of us, but we got through it. I don't think kindergarten should be a stressful experience for any child. However, the pressure to read at age five or younger is becoming the norm. It's true, some children are ready to learn at a young age, but others need additional time because developmentally, they aren't ready. Studies such as those by Suggate, Schaghency, and Reece (2013) show us that eventually the children who learn to read later catch up to the rest just fine.

The study done by Suggate et al. (2013) in New Zealand is very telling. Their study examined children who learned to read at age five and another group who learned to read at age seven. Their findings revealed that the seven-year-old children eventually caught up to the five-year-old children in their reading skills. Most importantly they found that the seven-year-old children had greater reader comprehension when compared to the five-year-old children. Perhaps this is because the older children were given more time to play and develop their imaginations? The study said that more research was needed to investigate this outcome. One thing is certain: the study showed that by age ten the reading fluency of both groups was the same, yet the children who learned to read at an older age had greater reading comprehension (both groups were tested at age ten). This study is just one that may help us better understand that the push to have children learn to read early is not necessary to their academic success in the long run.

Whether they learned to read at age five or at age seven, according to this study, by age ten all the children had the same reading fluency. The children who learned to read at age seven had a greater advantage in life though. Their reading comprehension skills were better. This is a crucial detail. If a child can read, but lacks understanding of the material being read, then their reading does not have meaning or purpose. All the children in this study had reading comprehension skills, the difference was that the children who learned to read at an older age had *greater* reading comprehension skills. The reason for better reading comprehension in the children who learned to read at an older age is unknown. There are some, including Schoning and Witcomb (2017) who believe the explanation for the older children having greater reading comprehension is that these children were provided with more time to play and explore the world before learning to read.

This is not to say that all learning related to reading should cease in preschool. Quite the contrary. There are many activities contained in this book that are focused on letter identification LEGO and letter writing skills, which are pre-reading skills important for preschool children to learn. Children can focus on learning letters in preschool, rather than learning to read. Focusing on letter identification and letter writing skills, while involving play activities in this learning process, is helpful to their cognitive development.

Learning to read in preschool is not crucial to a child's overall life success either. In fact, many experts on the subject of raising successful children do not cite early reading skills as a predictor of success in adulthood (Martin, 2017; Gillbert, 2017; Wojcicki, 2019). However, reading books to your children at a young age is correlated with their future academic success (Eckart, 2017).

Read books to your children and read to them often. If they are ready to learn to read, then teach them. If they aren't ready, don't push them. Let them play and develop. The reading skills will come much easier when they are ready to learn.

While this book emphasizes play activities, I must stress that reading to your child is just as important as play-time. Children should have books read aloud to them every single day. When books are read aloud to children on a regular basis, they acquire greater language skills, executive function skills, and study skills (Eckart, 2017).

The Developmental Skills that Play Impacts

Play helps with the development of various skills. The NAEYC (2009) cites that play helps children develop self-regulation, language, cognition, and social skills. These are just some of the skills that play can help children develop. There are far too many to list. If you can think of a skill, there is likely a play activity that can help children to develop that skill.

Play affects all four major areas of childhood development: physical, social, emotional, and cognitive. Physically, play can help children with the development of fine and gross motor skills. Different play activities help with the development of different skills. For example, a child playing with LEGO bricks is developing their fine motor skills. This means that they are synchronizing their eyes with their hands and fingers to complete a specific task. The more this skill is used, the more it develops. Playing with LEGO bricks can also help with the development of imaginative skills, construction skills, planning skills, and problem-solving skills. If they are playing with LEGO bricks with other children, they are also developing social skills such as cooperation, group planning, and leadership skills.

Another example is a child riding a scooter. When they are riding a scooter, the child is using their gross motor skills. They are improving this gross motor skill each time they ride. This activity will also help the child develop balance, hand-eye coordination, and focus.

Every play activity has benefits, some more than others. It is helpful for parents to seek out play activities for their child that are rich in developmental benefits. Providing children with a variety of developmental activities that affect a wide range of skills is beneficial. If they are only focused on activities that affect their fine motor skills, but fail to use their gross motor skills, then there will be an imbalance and deficit in their development. The activities in this book provide a variety of developmental and educational benefits. The goal is to let children play, so that they can learn and develop naturally, using numerous types of activities.

The Stages of Play and Why They Matter

Mildred Patten developed a theory about the stages of play that she published in her dissertation in the late 1920s. Her theory has been utilized by many clinicians and other professionals since its publication. These stages are widely accepted regarding socialization and how people learn to play with their peers as they age, develop, and mature.

It is helpful to understand these stages of play so that you can understand that babies interacting with one another in play is not normal. Interactive play doesn't typically happen until they are older. Understanding what kind of social play is generally expected at a particular age is helpful to parents and early childhood professionals. They can facilitate the type of play that aligns with the child's age and stage of development. Having a playdate and trying to get babies to share toys and interact through play can leave a parent frustrated if they don't understand that babies have not acquired those social skills and level of maturation.

The stages of play provide us with general guidelines regarding when children typically begin to socially interact and how they change their play methods as they mature and age. Next are the six stages of play, as developed by Mildred Patten. I have provided additional explanation to help you greater understand each stage.

Unoccupied Play

This play begins at birth. Some of the earliest signs of unoccupied play might be an infant making cooing noises or blowing bubbles with their saliva. You may see a baby randomly kicking their legs or flailing their arms. This is their method of play. It may appear random or meaningless to us, but it is how babies play. This is also how they learn. They are learning how to work their arms and legs. They are learning that they can make noises and that those noises can cause reactions.

Solitary Play

This type of play begins in infancy or while the child is a toddler. This is when they play on their own without noticing other children nearby. They may have a child sitting right next to them playing with blocks, while they are also playing blocks, yet neither child pays any attention to the other. They are focused on themselves and their own play. This type of play is also referred to as independent play. We actually engage in solitary play our entire lives, but it is during our earliest years that this type of play initially emerges. As we age, we can still participate in this type of play and we should from time to time. For example, working on model cars or building dollhouses can be solitary play or a solitary hobby that we enjoy as adults. Just because we mature to the next level of play doesn't mean we have outgrown the previous types of play. We can still participate in these earlier learned types of play, and we should as they are still healthy ways of playing.

Onlooker Play

Onlooker play typically begins when children are toddlers. This is play that involves watching others play. They are observing others who are playing, and they may ask questions about these children. They show interest in the children and their play, but they don't join in. This type of play is more of an observation of others playing and not an active participation. They are learning as they are observing. They are watching and processing what the children are doing. Someday they may put their observations into practice, but while engaged in onlooker play, they are merely observers and not participants. This type of play is not exclusive to toddlers; however, that is the age when this type of play begins. Some older children may engage in onlooker play because they are shy, or they may be trying to figure out the rules of the game being played. Some adults engage in a great deal of onlooker play when they regularly attend football games as spectators.

Parallel Play

This type of play usually begins when children are toddlers, approximately ages two to three. Parallel play is exactly as it sounds. It is children playing side by side with other children without having social interactions. In parallel play they are paying attention to what other children are doing around them, even though they may not be interacting with them. This differs from solitary play, which is play in which the child is not observant of the others around them. Parallel play involves playing alone, alongside other children, while also observing what the other children are doing. This type of play occurs without social interactions or communications between the children.

Associative Play

Associative play begins around the ages of three or four. In this type of play children begin interacting with one another. This is when social play begins. Children will finally become more interested in playing with the children around them rather than the toys. This is when they first get to experience social interactions and learn how to get along with other children while playing. This type of play typically doesn't have rules or organization, it is merely children playing together without structure. They will talk to one another and even play with the same toys together when they have reached the associative play stage.

Social Play or Cooperative Play

This stage goes by either name: social or cooperative play. This stage begins between the ages of four and six. In this stage of play children being to play more cooperatively. They may have rules or structure in their play that they implement. Children also support one another in this stage of play. For example, one child may be struggling to use the monkey bars, so another child helps show them how to do it successfully and may even help hold up their friend to grab the bars. Role play is also common during this stage. They will take on roles or characters and act them out through play. This stage of play is highly beneficial to children as they learn how to socially interact with their peers. It is in this stage that they learn social skills such as cooperation, rule following, taking turns, and problem solving.

The Importance of Cooperative Play

The sixth stage of play, known as social or cooperative play, is fundamental to social development during childhood. When children are not given the opportunity to play with other children during the critical ages of four to six because they are at a preschool where workbooks and academic teachings are the focus, then their social development suffers. Children need to be provided with the opportunity to have free play time with other children, so that they can naturally develop cooperative play skills. *These social skills are just as important as any academic learning.* The ability to understand their peers, relate to them, and interact with them, will develop normally when they have played with other children and learned social skills through their play.

Cooperative play skill development requires time and space to free play with peers. If play is limited to 15-minute recess time twice a day and no other free play time is allowed for a child during these ages, then their social development will likely suffer. Therefore, playing with other children outside of a school setting is imperative. If they are in a structured school environment all day and then they transition to sports activities and dance classes where more instruction is provided *and not playtime*, then they will not get the amount of social playtime needed for their development. Free play time for children ages four to six is especially crucial, as this is when they develop cooperative play skills and essentially learn to interact with their peers on common ground.

PART II

100+ Child Development Play Activities

Part II of this book contains 100+ play activities. There are a wide variety; Some are educational toys that my kids love, while others are manipulatives that were popular at our preschool. Still others are Pinterest types of activities that involve a certain amount of effort. I didn't want to focus on just one category because I believe there should be balance in utilizing each of these types of activities with our children. If we try to engage them with preschool manipulatives 100% of the time, they will get bored. Using activities from each of these categories, including DIY projects, educational toys, and preschool manipulatives will help children to be readily engaged in these activities *because of the variety.*

The Pinterest style projects contained in this book are easy enough for any parent to do. You do not need to be crafty or creative. The ability to follow some directions and perhaps print some printables found online is all that is needed to do these projects. The slime may be the most complicated of the projects, but even my seven-year-old was able to do this project, so it should be easy enough for you too.

The educational toys included in this book are all toys that we own. I purchased each of these items for my children to enhance their developmental skills and cognitive abilities. This book contains the best preschool educational or developmental toys that my kids love and use often. I am sponsored by no one. Therefore, I can provide my personal insight on these toys and activities based on my own experiences as to what delighted my children, versus someone who has been paid to promote specific toys. Nobody has compensated us in any way, nor have we been given any free toys, ever. The promotion of these toys is purely for the benefit of other families, so that they too can discover fun educational toys that will benefit their children developmentally.

I am not sponsored by any store or retail venue. I mention specific stores to purchase items to help readers in finding the items. I am cost conscious, which is why the Dollar Tree, Walmart, and Amazon are mentioned most often. It is not that I think everyone should shop at these locations exclusively. I am merely trying to help you, the reader, save money and to know exactly where I purchased the items myself.

The preschool manipulatives featured in this book come from either our personal home or were used at our preschool. Most are from our preschool. I was an active volunteer at my twin's preschool and was able to see firsthand what activities and manipulatives were most popular among the children. Therefore, I am featuring only manipulatives that my children enjoyed using. If there was a manipulative in the classroom that my kids didn't like or didn't enjoy, then I did not include it in this book. Having developmental benefits from an activity or manipulative is wonderful, but if the kids don't like it, then it is worthless in my opinion. Learning at the preschool level should be fun. Therefore, the manipulatives should be fun and engaging.

Every child is different, so your child may not love every activity presented in this book. That's ok. Your kid doesn't need to love everything. Finding even a handful of activities that can become a regular part of their playtime is great! Each activity has at least several developmental benefits. Therefore, if you find a handful that your child loves and wants to do on a regular basis, then you are on the right track. You do not need to provide all the activities in this book to your child. That is not the intention of this book. If you do, then you are super parent of the year, and I need to personally meet you so that I can learn from you! If you are a normal parent like the rest of us, then just pick out the activities that you are drawn to and that you think your child would enjoy doing.

Enjoying the activity is the most important factor, because children learn best when they enjoy doing something. Playtime should be enjoyable and fun! What you may find is that some of the manipulatives that you would think are boring, are very engaging for a preschooler. Don't judge an activity based on whether *you* think it would be fun. What matters is whether *the child* thinks it is fun, they engage in the activity, and are focused while playing. If they are, they will benefit in building developmental skills.

1 DIY Puppet Show

Supplies Needed

☐ Tension curtain rod that will fit your doorway
☐ various decorations for the puppets
☐ paper lunch sacks   ☐ glue
☐ markers   ☐ scissors
☐ construction paper   ☐ a sheet to create your stage

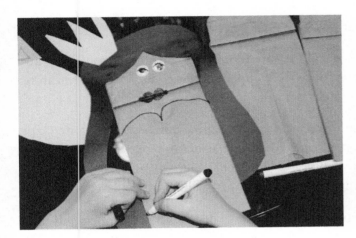 

This is a do-it-yourself puppet show! If you own some puppets you can incorporate them into your show as well. Your stage is quite easy to create. For a few dollars at Walmart you can pick up a tension curtain rod for your doorway. Measure the doorway you would like to use before going to Walmart, so you know the size of tension rod that you need. You will twist open the curtain rod until it fits firmly inside the doorway. No hardware is needed! Then you toss a lightweight sheet over the curtain rod and your stage is set! You can always make a sign to affix to the sheet that announces the name of your theatre or stage. Feel free to decorate your stage area and include the kids in the process. This helps them use their creativity skills to assist you in making the perfect stage for their puppets to perform.

In my photos you may see that I hemmed some fabric to make our stage curtain. I had some extra fabric to use for this project. We utilized a tension curtain rod between the doorway, which makes it easy to store the puppet stage. We simply roll up our curtain around the rod and it goes in our crafting closet between uses.

To make the puppets you need to decorate paper lunch sacks. The examples shown are some my kids and I created together one afternoon. They had fun creating them and they came up with the ideas for the puppets. They chose their puppets based on the story that they wanted to retell, which was Rapunzel.

This is a great activity to help them put their planning skills into practice. Creating the puppets using their scissors, glue, and markers utilizes their fine motor skills.

Once they have their puppets and the stage is in place, it is time to create a play! For young children, it is very difficult for them to create a story from scratch and then work together to perform the production. This is a lot to ask of small children. A better way to approach this activity is to have them think of a story that they know well that they are able to retell using their puppet characters. Once they have decided on the story, then they can figure out which puppet will be a particular character. This too is not easy for small children, so you can guide them in the process. This sort of directed play helps them learn how to do it themselves for future play.

You will need to set some basic rules for your puppet playtime:

1. The first rule is that puppets are not allowed to fight. When children don't know what to do with the puppets, they resort to puppet fighting. This is not helpful because usually one or both of the puppets gets destroyed in the process.

2. Another rule is that they must speak loudly so that their audience can hear them.

3. A third rule is that puppets will get a puppet time-out if they are too rowdy. This means the child can't play for a set time period. Allow them to play again, once the puppet has served its time-out (meaning the child sat out of puppet playtime as well).

4. A fourth rule is that they stick to the storyline that everyone selected. Killing off characters or attacking other puppets is not helpful nor is it playing cooperatively. This is what often happens when children decide to go their own direction with the script. Killing off other characters or puppets creates hurt feelings and an end to certain children participating, since some puppets will no longer have a role.

Help the children retell the story they want their puppets to act out before they do it with the puppets and their stage. Having them retell the story helps them to understand the progression of the story before they get started. It is not an easy process for young children so help them when needed. It is a good practice for story recall and their cognitive development. They are also learning while using their imaginations to re-create the story in their own way using the puppets that they made. It won't be a perfect process, but it is a fun learning activity!

2 Pour Method for Artwork on Canvas

Supplies Needed

☐ paint tarp or plastic to go under the artwork in progress
☐ Gallery wrapped canvases   ☐ water
☐ art smocks/old t-shirts   ☐ a hair dryer or two
☐ acrylic paint   ☐ cups

We did this art project as a playdate at our house. It was a success! And even small toddlers, ages two to three-years-old were able to participate with just a little help.

I asked all the Moms to bring a gallery wrapped canvas for their child to do their artwork. You can find them almost anywhere. Walmart, Ross, Hobby Lobby, Michaels, or any craft store will typically have gallery wrapped canvases for sale. For my daughter and niece to participate in this play date art project I purchased a five-pack of 11" by 14" canvases at Ross for $9.99. I also had an additional larger canvas on hand for my daughter Brielle to create a piece of artwork for our playroom. Every Mom came with a canvas in hand of whatever size they chose. "Gallery wrapped" simply means that you can't see the staples on the sides of the canvas. The canvas material is wrapped completely around the front and sides of a wood frame, so that the staples are on the back. No frame is needed, and the sides of the canvas can be painted. These canvases can hang on the wall exactly as they are!

The paint for this project is acrylic, so it stains and is permanent. We diluted the paint with water, but nevertheless, it will stain, so I had all the kids wear smocks or old t-shirts. It works best if parents can work with the children one at a time to assist them. Working with the children one-on-one helped us to contain the mess, and we provided them with basic instructions as they created their artwork.

Some instructions for the kids included directing them to pour the paint onto their canvas and then use the blow dryer to move the paint on the canvas. No paint brushes are needed! They get to be as creative as they want and use the colors as they so desire. Each canvas art piece turns out unique and is a work of cool artwork!

Allowing children to create their own work of art helps their creativity bloom and they gain confidence in their abilities in the process.

The acrylic paint was mixed in clear cups with water for diluting. The kids were instructed to select their colors. I purchased the cheapest acrylic paints at Walmart. There is no need for high-quality acrylics for this project, so save your money. For small canvases I recommend using only three colors for a couple of reasons. For one thing, when they use too many colors, they all start blending into the color of mud (brownish gray) on the canvas. It is best to use one color at a time, dry it a bit and then pour the next color onto the canvas. The paints were mixed with half paint and approximately half water. I like using vibrant colors because they show up better on the canvases. If the paint is not diluted it won't move on the canvas. It will just sit as a blob undiluted. Water helps the movement happen. More water makes the paint more diluted, which means weaker colors. This is why I selected vibrant colors of acrylics for this project.

After the kids had the appropriate smock or t-shirt on and they chose their three colors, they were handed one of the cups of diluted paint. Children could pour whatever amount they wanted onto their canvas. Some were extra cautious and only poured a dab, so I told them it was alright if they wanted to pour more. Others start dumping rather than pouring, so I had them slow down and pour a little less. It really doesn't matter much though. It you are concerned about your child pouring too much then you can divide the diluted paint into Dixie cups, so they have less to pour. If a piece of artwork gets over-blended and looks like mud the simple solution is to let it dry and then work over it. Acrylic goes over acrylic quite nicely.

If you want a particular color for the background, then paint the entire canvas that color and let it dry before you have your child begin the pouring method.

They use the hairdryer to move the paint on their canvas. They can experiment with the dryer further away and then closer to the canvas. Both methods will provide different results. I used a medium to cool setting. I did not use any hot settings, since it was already sweltering outside. Pouring and drying continues until the work of art is complete! We like to pour one color at a time, move it around with the dryer and then let it dry. They can pour all the colors and then use the blow-dryer, but it tends to turn into mud if there is too much mixing. Using the blow dryer between each layer of paint, allowing each layer to mostly dry before pouring the next color, tends to create the best effect, in my personal experience.

As I mentioned previously, three colors work best for the small canvases. If you use a larger canvas, like the canvas shown on the previous page, then you can use more colors. The painting was done by my daughter Brielle at this playdate. She was four years old when she made this work of art. We hung it in our playroom after the playdate.

This is an easy, fun, and creative play activity for young children. Supervision and help are required for this activity. Anytime kids use acrylics for a project they should be supervised. Unless you don't mind stained furniture, floors, and clothing.

You can see more photos from this art playdate on my website www.LivingJoyDaily.com. In the search bar at the top of the website use the words "Art Play Date" and the posting will come up for you.

3 Let's Pretend to Clean!

Supplies Needed

☐ Kid-safe cleaning tools from the Dollar Tree or another discount store

Kids like to copy what they see adults doing. Whether it is their parent, babysitter, or their preschool teacher, they watch when cleaning is happening. They watch, they learn, and they want to do it themselves! Kids model our behavior. This is a good one for them to model and practice. You can spend money on purchasing play cleaning tools from toy makers like Melissa and Doug. We have some of those at our house and our kids are still using the play broom five years later.

Another way to get cleaning tools that kids can use is to head to the Dollar Tree. Each of the items shown are from the Dollar Tree. I paid $5 total and my kids have spent a great deal of time playing with these cleaning tools. They can really clean with them too! I don't expect them to actually clean with these tools, but it is good practice for them.

This is a great role play activity that many kids like to do. They get to play out what it would be like to be the one caring for the home and keeping it clean. It is part of imaginative play and is important to development. They don't need to be toy cleaning tools, these soft bristle brushes and tools work just as well for their playtime. Just be sure that you give them tools that are safe, like the ones shown here that my five-year-old twins use for pretend cleaning. It was only $5 for all five of these items, which have provided hours of imaginative play for them. They use these tools when they play restaurant as well. Somebody must clean up after the customers leave and the restaurant needs to be tidied up.

It is fun to see them playing in a way that will serve them well later in life. **A great deal of play is helping children prepare for real life as adults.** It's also helpful when the activity doesn't cost much.

We also have small handheld vacuums for our kids to use. I purchased two of them when Walmart was selling dorm-room supplies at the time. They were under $20 each and they have been amazing! When the kids spill cereal in the kitchen, I tell them to go to the pantry and get their little vacuums out. They literally run to the pantry racing one another to see who can clean it up first. They have been using these small hand-vacs since they were about 3 years old. It may be play for them, but it is helpful to me too! It is a win-win!

4 Easy and Fancy Watercolor Cards

Supplies Needed

☐ Watercolor crayons
☐ blank cards

☐ paint brush
☐ a cup of water

If you want your child to look like a great painter with very little skill, then this project is right up your alley. It is a great activity that helps children with their fine motor skills, creativity, and planning skills. This is one we have done numerous times over the years.

The discovery that helped make this activity happen in our household involved finding watercolor crayons at Michaels. I found them by chance while browsing one day, killing a few minutes before preschool pickup. Michaels and Hobby Lobby are the places I like to go and browse when I get some free time. Sometimes it is Target, but either way, I end up in the craft section looking at what is new on the market and thinking of ideas to use them with my kids.

These watercolor crayons are amazing! Your child simply draws a picture and then they use water on a paintbrush over it to make the watercolor effect. It is so cool! Their simple crayon drawing turns into a watercolor masterpiece! We did this on blank cards. We picked up a pack of 50 blank cards at Michaels and used almost a dozen of them to make Easter cards for family and friends. It was a wonderful play activity for my kids. Brielle especially loved it since she is the household artist. All three kids participated and enjoyed drawing their own Easter artwork and then turning it into a work of watercolor art using a paintbrush and a little bit of water.

We have used these watercolor crayons on cardstock to create artwork to mail to family and friends. Our extended family lives mostly in other states, so it is nice to send some artwork from the kids when I mail family photos or school photos of the kids. It makes their playtime productive too! Win-win! They are very proud of their artwork, and when they are creating it for specific family members, they like to think about what that family member would like drawn or what colors the person may like best. This helps them to develop consideration for others, as this little activity can help them think about what others may be inclined to like.

5 Scoop and Pour

Supplies Needed

- ☐ Popcorn kernels
- ☐ funnels
- ☐ a scoop
- ☐ measuring cups
- ☐ plastic bowls

For my five-year-old twins this an activity they have been playing with every single morning for the past few weeks. It is remarkable how something so simple can be so entertaining. This simple set up is for scooping and pouring. You can use other items such as dried beans, but we prefer the popcorn kernels. They make a noise when poured that my kids like to hear. This activity is sensory based. It also makes good use of their fine motor skills. They also learn about pouring, measuring, and estimation.

Kids get to experiment with this activity. It becomes a science and math experiment in one activity. For example, they may think that they can use the funnel, and everything will fit into one of the small bowls, but they quickly learn that the amount is more than they estimated. They must get another container to fill. The playtime becomes a time of experimentation and learning. They want to see how much can fit in one container, which funnels work the fastest, and how high they can pour without the kernels bouncing out of the bowl and onto the floor. These are just a few of the experiments I have observed my children doing with this scoop and pour set-up.

Once again, the Dollar Tree came in handy for another project. The set of funnels, set of measuring cups, dish pan, and scoop were from the Dollar Tree. The little bowls were extras I found in our Tupperware cabinet, and we had the popcorn on hand in our pantry. My cost for this project was $4 at the Dollar Tree. They have spent far more hours using this activity than I ever imagined!

There is also something about the sound of the popcorn pouring and the texture when they hand-scoop the popcorn that my kids really like. It is sensory play that also involves learning. The experiments with this scoop and pour activity seem to be endless for the mind of a preschool child!

6 The Best Play Dough Recipe

- ☐ Flour
- ☐ vegetable oil
- ☐ cream of tartar
- ☐ salt
- ☐ water
- ☐ food coloring
- ☐ a large pot
- ☐ stove
- ☐ gallon-size Ziploc bags

This is literally the best play dough recipe ever, and I have done quite a few. I have also experimented with a variety of different ingredients over the years. This is by far the best in my personal experience. It is soft dough, but not sticky like some others I have made. It also lasts for months upon months if stored properly. It is the cream of tartar that makes it last long, so don't leave it out of the recipe when you are making your project. This recipe is super cheap and makes plenty. You won't need to bother buying play dough ever again once you make this! You will wonder why you didn't make this sooner. It takes approximately five to ten minutes to make this play dough.

Ingredients:

- 4 cups of all-purpose flour
- 1 ½ cups of salt
- 3 tablespoons cream of tartar
- 4 cups of warm water
- ¼ cup of vegetable oil
- Food coloring (optional)

In a large cooking pot, you will need to combine the flour, salt, and the cream of tartar. After you have mixed all these ingredients completely you can then add the water and oil.

Heat the ingredients in the large pot on the stove on medium heat. Mix continually. Once it has thickened and begins to form into a ball, remove from heat.

Put into the Ziploc bags and add food coloring. You can have your kids kneed the play dough in the bags to get the food coloring completely distributed on the dough. Using bags keeps their hands from getting dyed. This is also a great play activity. My kids played with the dough and dye in the bag for at least a half hour. It took me about 2 minutes to distribute the dye, but for them it was a fun way to play and a great sensory activity.

Once it is completely cool and the food coloring is evenly distributed on the dough it is ready for play dough playtime! Be sure to store in Ziploc bags, removing as much air from the bags as you can before zipping them closed. This will help the play dough last longer.

7 Play Dough Flower Garden

☐ Play dough ☐ flower stems ☐ small flowerpots

This creative activity helps kids use their imagination, design skills, and fine motor skills. All three of my kids loved this activity and were asking for more floral stems, even though between the three of them we had over 20 stems to utilize. This play activity is fun, and the kids were so proud of their finished work.

I purchased small flowerpots for this project. We also used empty Play-Doh containers, as these plastic containers were the perfect size to use as flowerpots for their arrangements. I am glad I saved them rather than tossing them out with the dried-up Play-Doh. I purchased 4-5 floral bunches and cut them apart. When you cut them make sure that none of the wire is sticking out or it can be a hazard for children. I used a utility scissors that pinched the plastic closed as I cut each piece, so no wire from the stems was felt or seen. If you do see any wire, you can always use Duct tape at the end to seal it off. First and foremost, safety is most important.

We used our homemade play dough from activity #6. Because we made the entire batch there was plenty of leftover play dough to fill many pots for this activity. They used the flower stems to create their own flower arrangements with play dough in the bottom of the pots holding everything in place. The more colors and types of flowers, the better! Let them get creative and their flower arranging skills will blossom. It is a good way to help them develop their skills in design, order, and balance, as they work to make the flowers arrangements look how they envision in their own mind. For my boys they were going for more of a wild and fun jungle look. They wanted more leafy greens to use, so I will keep that in mind the next time I am shopping. My daughter, on the other hand, was going for a bridal bouquet look. After several attempts, they all accomplished their goals.

In most cases, even such a simple activity does not turn out the way they want the first time. That's why play is so important. **Play is a way for kids to practice their skills and they get many attempts to try again without any pressure to perform. This is how their creative skills bloom; when they are given space and time to explore their imagination and put it into practice.**

8 Play Dough Cookie Cutter Play

My kids enjoy making cutout cookies, but I don't want to bake as often as they would like to make them. They don't want to make them to eat. That's just a bonus to my kids. They really want to make cutout cookies so they can play with the dough, roll it out, and use the cookie cutters.

A great way to use play dough and get kids to practice their cookie making skills is by giving them mini rolling pins (I found some in the kitchen section at Walmart) and cookie cutters you already have on hand. You can always wash the cookie cutters and use them later for cookies. It is a good way to use what you already own.

This activity helps with their imagination, role play skills as they pretend to be chefs in the kitchen, fine motor skills, hand-eye coordination, and concentration skills. It requires focus and practice to get the dough rolled out to the correct thickness that the cookie cutters will work best, while the shape remains intact when removing the cutout shape from the counter. It is great practice in teaching little hands to be gentle and careful with something that is delicate. They learn as they work with the dough that if they rush or use too much force their play dough cookies break apart or lose their shape.

If you have cookie cutters in different shapes this is also a good time to help teach them about shapes like circles, rectangles, squares, ovals, etc. You can have them say the names of each shape as they cut them out. You can also have them group them into categories when they get multiples of each shape created. It can be a fun way to practice their shapes and their sorting skills as they are playing. They won't even realize it is learning time. For them it's just fun with play dough!

9 Dry Erase Board Fun

Supplies Needed

☐ Dry erase board and dry erase markers

This activity is simple, yet will keep your child entertained for extended periods of time, especially if you offer some direction on what to draw or what numbers and letters for them to practice writing. The reusable board can be used over and over again, just be sure they don't use any permanent markers, crayons, pens, or pencils on this board. This board is to be used with dry erase markers only.

Why a dry erase board? If you find that you are going through lots of paper with your creative child who is motivated to write or draw, this is a wonderful alternative to something more permanent. They get to draw imaginative pictures, shapes, and endlessly practice writing letters and numbers. Kids tend to prefer dry erase boards over chalk boards. I do, too. The squeak of a dry erase board is satisfying compared to the sound of chalk screeching on a chalkboard. Colors are also more vibrant on a dry erase board than chalk on a chalkboard. Chalks tend to be more muted in color. This is something to keep in mind when you are trying to decide between a dry erase board and a chalkboard.

You can pick up a variety pack of dry erase markers at Walmart, Target, the Dollar Tree, or any office supply store. You can get many different colors including fluorescents, primary colors, pastels, and more. This can make the drawing and writing even more fun and experimental. You don't need a huge dry erase board to hang on a wall, but you can always hang one on a playroom or activity wall if you so desire. Letting them practice drawing their letters and numbers in a seated position with the board on a flat horizontal surface rather than drawing against a wall is the best way for them to learn how to write correctly, as they are positioned properly for learning to write.

What I do with my kids for this activity is that I write something at the top of their board and then they practice copying it below. For example, as they were learning to write their names, I would write it once clearly at the top and then have them copy it below. They can use whatever colors they want and they can experiment making their name as big or as small as they want. The goal is to get them practicing writing their name, or whatever it is that they are practicing, while they are enjoying the activity.

A dry erase board is not exclusively for learning numbers, letters, and shapes alone. Children can use their imagination and create works of art using the dry erase board and dry erase marker. Using the board and markers helps develop their fine motor skills, creative skills, and writing skills. It is also an opportunity for them to practice and learn shapes, colors, numbers, and letters.

Telling the kids, a theme for the day when they pull out their dry erase boards is a good way to get them started. For example, if it's December you can have them draw Christmas trees with ornaments as their theme. Then you ask each child to count their ornaments out loud.

Drawing and writing are essential preschool activities that support children and their development of fine motor skills, language skills, and creativity. The more that they do this and enjoy it, the better their skills will develop naturally.

10 Play Dough Mats

Supplies Needed

☐ Play dough printable mats (or you can draw them yourself)
☐ laminating sheets
☐ play dough

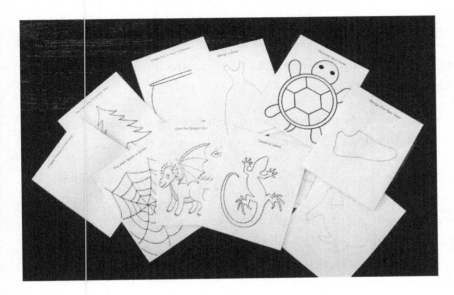

Play dough mats are laminated sheets that have simple designs. The designs help to ignite a child's imagination. It is up to kids to create and complete the design using play dough. In the photo you will find 3 simple designs that you likely can draw yourself. On my website you can find 12 designs for play dough mats that I created and are available as free printables. To download them, simply go to www.livingjoydaily.com. Find the search tool at the top of the website and enter the phrase "play dough mats."

The posting will appear, and you can print as many designs as you want. As always, they are free.

For additional designs, you can go to Pinterest and search similar key words. You will find other options, most of which are free to print.

Once you have printed the mats you need to laminate them. If you do not own a laminating machine, no worries, you can still laminate! Amazon, Walmart, and office supply stores all sell self-laminating pockets. These allow you to laminate without a machine. I have used these many times. Then I got smart and purchased an inexpensive laminator from Amazon. I have been using that same laminator for almost 10 years now. I buy refill laminating pouches from Amazon in boxes of 100, so I always have plenty on hand. Laminating is very easy with a machine. The human error is taken out the equation, so you don't have bubbles or wrinkles in your finished product. When you use self-laminating pouches, you have to be very careful and take your time so that you don't get bubbles, wrinkles, or creases. It is possible, but in the long run purchasing a laminator is easier than using the self-laminating pouches. The self-laminating pouches also tend to be quite expensive in comparison to laminating sheets used with laminating machines. Do a price comparison if you think you will use a laminator more than once or twice.

Once your mats are laminated, they are ready for use! They can be wiped clean after each use. Since the mats are laminated, they should last a long time. The other benefit of using play dough mats is that it keeps your table mess-free! In my case when my kids go off the mats, it's at least less mess.

Don't forget that you can make your own play dough for just a few dollars. Make sure you have a large batch for your kids to create their designs. Check out activity #6 for the best play dough recipe ever! This recipe provides plenty of play dough for several children to use the play dough mats and create their designs at the same time.

Play dough is a wonderful sensory tool to help children develop and learn. It has been the staple of early childhood play for decades and should be for decades to come. There are many skills that are developed while children use the play dough. For example, they are using problem solving skills as they try to figure out how to build a snowman without it toppling over. They are learning language skills as they talk about how they are using the play dough (i.e. I am squishing the dough between my finger, I am pounding it out flat). Rolling, squishing, shaping, and molding the play dough builds finger and hand strength. As they create different designs, they are developing their fine motor skills. They are also exploring their creative thought processes and imagination when they play with play dough.

Below is a list of household items that children can use to play with play dough (just be sure to provide them only if they are age appropriate for the child and they don't put these objects in their mouth).

- Bottlecaps
- Empty water bottles (for rolling)
- Laces for imprinting shapes on the play dough
- Combs for creating patterns on the play dough
- Straws
- Spoons
- Small plastic toy figures (that can easily be washed)
- Twigs and leaves
- Toy blocks (that can easily be cleaned, or you will regret it)

11 Fingerprint Animals

Supplies Needed ☐ Fingerprint ink pads (washable)   ☐ paper

This is a simple and fun project. It was a perfect activity for my seven-year-old daughter. She spent well over an hour creating her own animal and bug fingerprint designs. I created a sample sheet, so you have examples to utilize. You don't need to have any drawing skills to help your child with this project. Simply show them the designs on this page and let them create the fingerprint animals on their own! Even my five-year-old twins were able to create many of these simple designs.

The fingerprint inkpad set that we purchased was made by a company named Bess. This exact set can be found on Amazon and at Walmart. When we purchased this set of 20 it was under $10 (it's double layers of ink in the package, so you may only see 10 inkpads in photo, but it is indeed 20). We have done a lot of art projects with these ink pads and they are still producing plenty of ink for our fingerprint projects! These are washable, which means the ink easily comes off little fingers and won't stain their hands. I gave my kids wet wipes, so they could clean their fingers on their own as they created their projects. It was a low mess project compared to any paint projects we have completed.

You can see activity #12 for the developmental benefits of fingerprint art activities.

12 Fingerprint Artwork Printables

Supplies Needed

☐ Fingerprint ink pads (washable)

☐ printables

For this fingerprint artwork project, we used our set of 20 fingerprint ink pads that we purchased on Amazon for under $10. For the exact link to this product you can go to my blog www.livingjoydaily.com. Type in the phrase "fingerprint printables," where you will find these free printable sheets for your kids to create their own masterpieces using just their fingerprints and ink pads! The printables consist of a mason jar (which you fill with fingerprinted fireflies), a trike with a balloon bouquet (the balloons are made using fingerprints), and dandelions ready to blow in the wind. A fingerprint is needed at the end of each stem of the dandelion along with some blowing in the wind.

Fingerprint artwork is a great project for young children, including toddlers. It helps to strengthen their hand and finger muscles and develop their fine motor skills. It is also considered an emotionally calming sensory activity. This is a sensory activity because they are using the inkpads and the pads of their fingers. When children do this activity, they are being creative and using their imagination, which helps with their overall cognitive development. Creating the artwork using the printable sheets also helps children with their focus and concentration skills. It requires some effort on their part to place their fingerprints in the correct spot to make the artwork.

13 Stamping Cards

Supplies Needed

☐ Fingerprint ink pads (washable)   ☐ blank cards   ☐ a letter stamp set

If you own the set of inkpads mentioned in the previous activities, then why not get some wooden letter stamps too! We picked up an entire set for under $5 at Walmart. You can also find plenty of stamp options at art supply stores such as Hobby Lobby and Michael's.

This stamping activity can help children with their letter recognition skills. It is also a good exercise in concentration and focus as they work hard to line up the stamps, so that their words turn out correctly. Their fine motor skills are also put into practice, along with their creativity skills.

We decided to use our stamps on this particular day to create hand-made thank you cards. We have a bin in our craft closet that contains blank cards and envelopes so that the kids can create hand-made cards anytime. My twins will begin kindergarten in the fall, and they are just beginning to learn how to read and write. Using the stamps was a great way for them to practice letter recognition. I wrote "Thank You" on a piece of paper, so they knew what letters to look for and in which order they should be stamped. The rest was up to them. They did it! Charlie almost mixed up the n and the k in thank. However, he caught himself before the error was made. He was proud that he got it right the first time! This kind of small victory in stamping out simple words was confidence building for Charlie. **Creating small achievable play activities that build on their skills will in turn build a child's confidence.**

This is also a great way for children to practice their name. They can use the stamps to stamp out their name on a piece of paper over and over again, much like they would do if they were writing. This will help them better remember the letters and the order in which the letters are spelled out in their name. It is also a lot more fun than simply writing. Stamping is fun and helps children build their fine motor skills.

14 Wikki Stix

Supplies Needed

☐ Wikki Stix and Wikki Stix cards

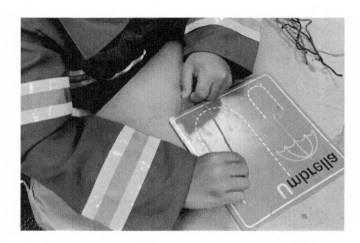 

This is a manipulative that my twins used many times at preschool this past school year. They liked it so much that we purchased a travel Wikki Stix set for our summer road trips. I found the kit on Amazon and it was not an expensive manipulative to purchase. Thank you to our preschool director for introducing us to this manipulative and many others that have helped my twins learn and play simultaneously!

Wikki Stix are made of hand-knitting yarn and are coated with a non-toxic, food grade wax. This makes them sticky enough to hold in place when you position them on a Wikki card. They are bendable, moldable, and make for a great sensory learning activity. They are just plain fun to play with too!

Wikki Stix can be twisted, shaped, tied, looped, and more. They are a wonderful tool for fine motor development. Examples of Wikki Stix cards are shown in the photos. The cards are cardboard or plastic boards that the children use to apply their Wikki Stix. Some helpful cards for learning include those with numbers and letters. While the kids are playing with the Wikki Stix they are also learning their letters and numbers. If they aren't ready for letters or numbers just yet, then they can start with basic shapes. Wikki Stix are very helpful in preparing preschool-aged children for kindergarten as they hone their fine motor skills with this play activity.

Wikki Stix and Wikki Stix cards can be found on Amazon. That is where I found the best prices for these products for our own personal purchase of Wikki Stix.

15 Sand Letter Drawing

☐ Bin and colored sand

Kids love to play in sand. It is a sensory experience that is soothing to many children. They like to experiment how it feels when it sifts through their fingers or how it falls as they scoop and drop handfuls of sand a foot above the bin.

What the brain practices it learns. This sand letter activity is used to help children learn their alphabet and numbers. It can also be used to help them learn their shapes. You can either draw the letters that you want them to practice on a piece of paper, or if you have letter and number flash cards you can use those as well. For example, you can set out the flash card for the letter B. It shows the capital B and the lower-case b on the card. Ask the child to write both versions of the B in the sand using their finger. This activity helps to stimulate language development as they write out letters and words. It also supports their brain development in remembering the motions that are involved in making specific letters. Those same motions are used when they will someday write the words on paper.

This is a good activity for children who can't write yet but have the ability to use their fingers to draw shapes. It is also helpful practice for those children who are in the process of learning to write their letters. This tool is a fun way to practice writing letters as they play in the sand. Of course, they will play with the sand as they write, as that is all part of the process of learning. **Play is learning.**

Provide some directions to get them started. For example, by asking them to write certain letters and showing them on paper or a flash card. Then let them try it out for themselves and allow them to play with the sand in the process. This is how children learn best. It is also how their creativity can flourish. **Free play is needed in addition to directed play.**

We have found and purchased colored sand at Walmart, Hobby Lobby, and the Dollar Tree. You can use a tray similar to the one in the photo if you have one. An inexpensive option, if you don't own a tray like this, is a plastic dish pan from the Dollar Tree. They work for a variety of the activities found in this book, so the dishpan is a helpful item to have on hand.

16 Train in a Tin

☐ Train in a Tin

My boys are obsessed with trains. I think obsessed is an understatement. We were given a fancy train set for Christmas. It is one that is to be looked at and not necessarily played with by children. It even has smoke that comes out the top of the train engine. It is so cool! It is also only used at Christmastime around our tree. When the Christmas tree came down it was also time for the train to be put away, and our son Charlie cried and cried. I relented and put it around the coffee table for a few more weeks after the decorations came down. Did I mention that they had a train table and lots of trains in their playroom that they could play with anytime?

The train in a tin is an awesome train play activity and a great alternative to the large train play sets. With our train table in the playroom I glued down the wooden tracks, because when we initially purchased the table, they were still toddlers. They would throw the pieces around the room and I struggled to put it back together more times than I care to remember. Now that they are old enough to put the tracks back together themselves, they can't because they are glued down permanently. That's ok though! The train in a tin is a perfect solution because everything fits inside the storage tin and they can build their own train track system anytime they want. It is small, which is also good for fine motor skill development. Precise coordinated finger movements are required to put the tracks together, which challenges their skills, making it good for early childhood development. This is a great cognitive learning activity, much like putting a puzzle together. If your children or students are like my twins and love trains, then they will think it's more fun than learning. But we all know learning is still occurring!

This is another learning toy that we found at our preschool. We purchased our own train in a tin from Amazon for under $10 (there is no guarantee on the current price, but it shouldn't be an expensive toy to purchase). It is another great find for both preschools, daycares, and home use!

17 Shape Shuffle and Wooden Pattern Blocks

☐ Shape Shuffle STEM Game

This shape shuffle game is another manipulative from our preschool. We also have a set at home. The Shape Shuffle is a STEM activity. STEM stands for science, technology, engineering, and math. This activity helps children develop their problem-solving skills while also engaging their creativity. This activity set comes with small plastic shapes and double-sided cards. The cards have objects for them to build using the shapes from the kit. Some are simple for younger children; some are a bit harder and are intended for older preschool children. This is a great activity to help children learn their shapes and work on their geometry skills. This manipulative is priced inexpensively on Amazon. It should be a staple play activity in every preschool, childcare center, and home. This manipulative also goes by other names such as wooden pattern blocks and attribute blocks.

If they go through all the cards or get bored with the cards after months of using them, then have them create their own cards. This is a great way to get them thinking and creating. Give them some blank paper and show them how to trace the shapes. They can trace the shapes and create their own shape shuffle cards. If they turn out good, then laminate them for future use. You can also find free printable sheets for these shapes on Pinterest. There are bloggers who have created their own shape sheets, which they have made available for others to print at no cost.

18 Domino Matching

☐ A set of dominoes

Our family plays Mexican Train Dominoes. This is a fun game to play with family and friends. Children can generally start playing this game at ages four or five with some assistance. It is very helpful for learning math and counting skills. My five-year-old twins are just now learning how to play this game on their own, without assistance. You can find the instructions for this game by Googling "Mexican Train Dominoes." You will need a set of dominoes that go all the way to double twelves. You may not understand what "double twelves" means, but you will if you start looking at different sets of dominoes to purchase your own set.

Smaller domino sets are great for preschool learning. A good way for preschool children to practice matching is by using a set of small dominoes. You can find a variety of domino sets for sale online. They don't all have numbers on them. This particular set shown in the photo has different models and colors of cars. My son Alex is matching up the dominoes on each end with dominoes that have cars that match. You can also do this with numbered dominoes or dominoes that have letters. This activity helps with their fine motor skills as they line up each domino precisely. They are also learning how to identify and match like-items, numbers, colors, and shapes. This activity also helps them develop their problem-solving skills. They can play this alone or with friends. Either way they are learning as they play!

19 Numerical Balance and Playing with Scales

Supplies Needed   ☐ Numerical Balance learning kit or a tabletop scale

This is a preschool learning activity that helps children learn about scales, balance, measurement, and numbers all at the same time! It also provides them with the opportunity to experiment and test the weight of items in this kit. Each letter is a different size and has a different weight. The higher the number, the larger it is, and the greater its weight. This toy measuring tool works through balance and will show children which numbers weigh more, based on the movement of the scale. They can also use multiple numbers at one time to create balance. This helps them with problem solving and math skills as they experiment with which numbers combined together will equal another number.

You can find this activity on Amazon using the search term "Number Balance." There are a variety of different types of number balance activities that can be found online. These numerical balance learning toys are STEM activities. This means they are engaging in science, technology, engineering, and math in one activity.

My kids like to explore with scales in general. If you have a tabletop scale you can experiment with toys, books, and objects and which items weigh the most versus which weigh the least. For kids it is experimental play that is fun. They are learning and playing at the same time. Children enjoy playing with adult tools. We have a decorative table scale that I allow my children to use, so they play with ours quite often. When your kids go to play with your scale, remember that they are learning as they experiment with your scale. Sometimes we don't want them playing with our things because we don't want them broken (at least that is the case in our home). However, bringing out the scale and initiating play with them is a great way to teach them how it works and learn about weights and measurements at the same time. They will be bringing you dozens of items to weigh on the scale out of sheer curiosity. It is also a helpful activity in learning numbers. You can have them write down the weights of each item so they can compare the numbers and determine which weigh the most and which weigh the least. We do this at home when I have packages to mail. They want to get in on the action and see the scale at work! Something so simple can be a great learning experience for children.

20 Magnatabs

Supplies Needed

☐ Magnatabs toy

Magnatabs are a manipulative that help children with their hand-eye coordination and fine motor skills. They move magnets in these toys to create letters, numbers, shapes, etc. using a magnetic stylus. There are also free play Magnatabs toys. These allow kids to use their imagination to create designs, words, numbers, or letters using the magnets in the toy and a magnetic stylus (included with the toy).

Alex is using a numbered Magnatabs manipulative in the photo. This activity helps children learn their numbers while practicing holding a stylus, just like they would hold a pencil. This motion helps their brain remember and recall the motions needed for writing these numbers. Magnatabs can also be purchased as an alphabet toy, which can help children learn their letters and the muscle memory associated with drawing each letter.

The Magnatabs involve sensory-reinforced learning. Children like to hear the click every time a magnet slides into the correct place. It reinforces correct letter and number writing with the click of every magnet as it slides into place when they move the stylus correctly. This helps with their fine motor skills while also learning to master early penmanship.

21 Building with Giant Foam Blocks

Supplies Needed

☐ Set of Giant Foam Blocks

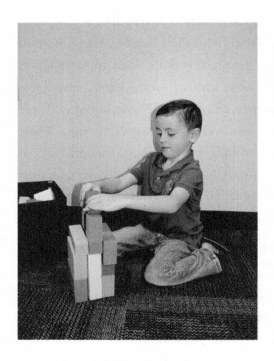

We had a set of small foam blocks for a while. I got tired of picking them up. My twins spent more time throwing them than building with them. They never liked to actually build with the small blocks. However, *giant* foam blocks are a game changer. Alex loves building with them, and he can do so for hours on end. My suggestion is to skip the small foam block purchase. There is a reason why you can find them so often on Facebook buy, sell, and trade pages. The giant foam blocks are what they want for building and creating. Truly, the bigger that they are, the more kids love them. **What child doesn't want to build something just so that they can knock it down? It's all about experimenting through play.** These foam blocks are perfect for that kind of play. They are soft, perfect for building, and create hours of fun. The small foam blocks tend to knock down too easily because they weigh next to nothing at all, making it difficult to build with them.

Giant foam blocks can help children develop their engineering, building, and problem-solving skills, while stimulating creative play. They also learn logical play and learning experiences because when they build, they learn what fits and works, and what does not.

You can find giant foam blocks on Amazon. Walmart also has them for sale on their website for good prices. Check out both sites to find the best current deals available.

22 Ribbon Play

☐ Ribbon Sticks

Oh, my goodness. These are the best. Kids love to play with these ribbon sticks. They are the kind you may have watched gymnasts use in previous Olympic games. I don't think they use them anymore. But why not? They are amazing. I even use them when I am playing with children. I used them every week when I taught music and movement classes at our preschool.

Ribbon sticks are something you can make or buy for a low price online. I was thinking about making a dozen for my preschool music classes when I searched for them on Amazon and realized I could buy them cheaper than I could make them. Done and done.

For our music classes I would play songs from various Disney movies such as "For the First Time in Forever" from the movie *Frozen* and "Part of Your World" from *The Little Mermaid*. This activity helps with their gross motor skill development. It is also helpful in giving children physical exercise. As they practice with the sticks, you can direct them to do zigzags, figure eights, and circles with their ribbons. This activity will also help develop their gross motor coordination and hand-eye coordination skills. When they twirl with the ribbons, they are also helping to develop balancing skills.

When you are using ribbon sticks with a group of children have them spread out so that they don't hit each other with their ribbon sticks. You can buy an entire set quite inexpensively, which is great for a class or playdate activity.

23 Math Cubes Pattern Play

Supplies Needed

☐ A set of Math Cubes

☐ printable pattern cards from Pinterest

Math Cubes can usually be ordered online for under $10 a set (however, there is no guarantee on this price). One place for downloading free Math Cubes' printables is on Pinterest. The pattern cards that you'll find there can help with children learning the AA, AB, ABA patterns, and more. On Pinterest you can also find pictures of objects that can be created with the Math Cubes, such as a camera. These cubes are wonderful because they can begin being used by two-year-old children (if they don't put them in their mouth, as they are a small hazard), yet there are activities for children upwards of 7 years old that can be found on Pinterest. Get started by purchasing a set and then downloading some age-appropriate printables online for your child to use with the Math Cubes.

Children are practicing their fine motor skills while using these Math Cubes. They also use their creativity when they free play with the cubes and make up their own designs. Other skills that can be further developed with Math Cube play include math, problem-solving, engineering, and patternmaking.

24 Pattern Beads

Supplies Needed

☐ Pattern beads   ☐ pattern bead cards

Pattern bead sets and cards can be found on Amazon and sold as kits. Just use the terms "pattern beads" and "learning" on Amazon to search for these kits. There are a variety of manufactures selling pattern beads online, but it is helpful to find bead sets that are sold with the pattern cards. This makes it easy, as no printing is needed. However, if you don't purchase the pattern cards, you can find printables on Pinterest.

Children learn by following the pattern cards. They learn about patterns, sequencing, recognizing order, and predictability though this beading activity. The activity also helps develop fine motor skills. They must focus and concentrate to get the beads threaded on the string, which also helps their hand-eye coordination development. This activity is a great one for helping children develop foundational skills that will help them in reading and math cognition.

Much like other activities in this book that include small objects, keep these items away from small children who will put the beads or strings in their mouth. These items are also a choking hazard.

25 Stained Glass Artwork

☐ Contact paper (or similar options described below)
☐ tissue paper
☐ tape

This activity is a fun one! It is not that much work and the results are beautiful! Especially knowing that the children created it makes it even more special. All three of my kids helped make this faux stained-glass artwork. I picked up a roll of clear laminate at Walmart. It was found in the section where kitchen items and shelf liners are sold. Yes, it makes for great shelf liner too! The adhesive is just the right amount of stickiness for this craft project.

We had a package of colored tissue paper on hand at home. We shredded a few different colors by hand. You can also buy shredded tissue, but we probably used only 20 cents of tissue paper by shredding our own. The shredding took about two minutes, and the kids enjoyed doing it.

To do this activity you will need to cut the amount of laminate that you would like to use. You can then remove the backing. I hung my top corners on the window first, by peeling just the corners back. Once it was hanging straight and taped in the top corners, I then removed the rest of the backing. I did this so I wouldn't get wrinkles in it when carrying it from the counter to the window without a backing on it. Once it is hung and the backing is removed make sure that all four corners are taped down. Then use a large kitchen mixing bowl to trace a circle on the laminate. This circle is where the kids will apply their tissue paper scraps to make the colorful stained-glass effect. Once they have completely covered the inside of the circle it is time to cut another piece of laminate to go over the work of art. Make sure it is sealed on the outside of the circle, all the way around. You can then remove it from the window and cut out the circle. Leave about an inch of clear laminate around the circle as this is what holds everything in place. If you cut into the tissue paper it will come apart, so avoid cutting into the tissue!

You can then hang it on a window. I suggest using a hole punch and a suction cup with a hook. We used a small suction cup with a hook that came from our sun catcher crafting supplies. If you have those on hand it makes it easy to hang this project as well.

This activity helps in developing creativity, planning, and problem-solving skills, as well as fine motor skills. Children must also follow instructions for this activity, which helps to develop listening and following verbal directions.

You can create different shaped faux stained-glass artwork. Simply draw the shape that you want to create on the laminate when it is hanging on the window. We drew a circle because it was easy to do. We have also created large Easter eggs and crosses with this activity. I drew the designs on the laminate for the kids using a Sharpie marker. They needed to stay within the lines in order to create the artwork. Having them work on staying within the lines when applying the tissue paper works their fine motor skills, concentration skills, and hand-eye coordination. Smaller children may need some assistance around the edges of the lines, but it is good practice of these skills for them, even with some assistance.

Creating lasting artwork that you can have for years to come is a wonderful way to make memories. The art will remind you of the precious time you spent together while you were creating the artwork with your children.

26 DIY Sequencing Puzzles

Supplies Needed

☐ Large popsicle sticks   ☐ markers   ☐ Duct tape

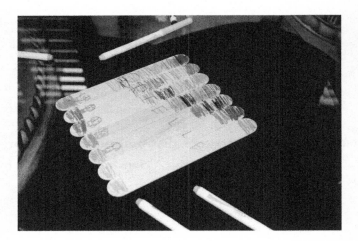

Your kids can create their own sequencing puzzles very easily. You will need large popsicle sticks from the crafting section at Walmart or from any craft store. They are cheap to buy.

You will need to help them by lining up 7-10 sticks and taping them together on one side using Duct tape. This will ensure that they stay together while your child is creating their sequencing puzzle, which you can help them create by drawing on the sticks. One way to get started and help them understand this concept is to have them write their name on the sticks; one letter per stick. Then they color the sticks and use their creativity to make them their own work of art. Once they are finished coloring, you can remove the Duct tape from the back. Your child now has their own sequencing puzzle!

This activity helps them to understand order and sequencing. It is also a good activity to let their imaginations go to work. They are not limited to their name alone. You can also help them do number sequencing. This would allow them to draw any picture that they want on the sticks, for example a ship or a car. Then they write the numbers at the bottom of each stick in order. If they can't write their numbers yet, then you can help by writing the numbers for them. Having numbers on the puzzle pieces (each popsicle stick is a puzzle piece) makes it more than just a regular puzzle, it is a sequencing puzzle. You can get more ideas for sequencing on Pinterest.

Children are using their fine motor skills in creating this activity. They are also engaging their creative thought processes to create a design for their puzzle. Their artistic skills are put into practice as they draw their design. When they play with the puzzle, they are engaging their cognitive skills and are learning about order and sequence.

27 Dinner Placemats

Supplies Needed

☐ Printable from www.livingjoydaily.com

☐ laminating sheets

For this activity, you can find the free printable placemat on my blog at www.livingjoydaily.com. Use the search terms "printable mat" and it should pop right up. If you'd rather, you can also have your child draw out the placemat instead of using the printable. Just use the photo and have them replicate the same place setting, so that the fork goes on the left and the knife and spoon on the right. This activity is to help them learn how to set a table properly. They learn where the silverware goes on each side of the plate. They also can customize and decorate each place setting for each member of the family. After they are completed, make sure each family member has their own placemat with their name on it. They are then ready to laminate. As I mentioned in an earlier activity, you can use self-laminating pouches or a laminating machine if you own one.

This activity helps children develop manners and etiquette. Once they are laminated, the placemats are reusable for each meal. They also wipe clean with a sponge or washcloth. This activity is also a good time to practice mealtime behavior and talk about table manners. Doing so while they are coloring their placemat is a good idea because they will hopefully remember your discussion when they see the placemat at future mealtimes. **Children tend to listen and absorb more than you realize when they are active.** Play and learning go hand in hand, so if you talk about mealtime manners while they are coloring and decorating the placemats, they are learning at the same time.

28 Beaded Bracelets

Supplies Needed

☐ Wood beads   ☐ crafting pipe cleaners

This activity is a good free play activity, but it can also be used to make bracelets and necklaces. The neat thing about using the pipe cleaners is that children can remake the bracelets anytime that they want.

We picked up a variety pack of wood beads in the crafting section at Walmart. Inspect the beads before purchase to ensure that their holes are large enough for the pipe cleaners to go through easily. Pipe cleaners can also be found in any crafting store.

Kids can use these beads to create patterns on the pipe cleaners. You can either draw on a piece of paper the color patterns for them to make or ask them to create their own patterns. It is always fun to see what they can come up with on their own, and they are usually very proud of their creativity and original ideas.

Using the pipe cleaners is easy. They slide the beads on and then twist and fold the ends to close the bracelet. The necklaces and bracelets can always be opened and untwisted, to be reworked into a new creation.

With this activity children also learn about measurements, as they discover what they need greater—or fewer—beads for their bracelet to fit around their wrist. They also use their fine motor skills to put the beads onto the pipe cleaners. For smaller children it often requires great focus and concentration to do this activity, which makes it more of a challenge for them. That is a good thing. **The greater the challenge that they can complete, the more they are building their developmental skills.** It is also good for strengthening finger and thumb muscles while also creating muscle memory associated with this fine motor task.

29 Sun Catchers

Supplies Needed

☐ Plastic sun catchers   ☐ paint   ☐ suction cups for windows

You can purchase plastic sun catcher craft activity kits at Walmart or at crafting stores such as Hobby Lobby and Michaels. They also have individual sun catchers for sale in the same section. We purchased the kit so that we got the paints and suction cups all at once. We purchased additional sun catchers at both Walmart and Hobby Lobby. Both stores, like many with craft sections, have displays filled with dozens of different sun catcher designs. I let my children pick out the ones that they wanted to paint.

This activity is a good one for mailing completed sun catchers to loved ones who live far away. They are lightweight and fit inside an envelope. Loved ones can hang them in their windows and think of their nieces, nephews, or grandchildren every time they look at the sun catchers. If you ever visit nursing homes, this is a nice small gift to bring to residents. They will love that small hands created these sun catchers just for them.

Children enjoy painting and decorating sun catchers. The paint for sun catchers does stain clothing, so be sure to protect surfaces and children's clothing. We have done this project at playdates we have hosted at our home. I used a plastic disposable tablecloth to protect my table, and then I provided old t-shirts for the kids to wear so they wouldn't stain their clothing. This activity uses their creativity, fine motor skills, planning skills, execution skills, and focus to stay within the lines.

30 Hopscotch

Supplies Needed

☐ Chalk and pavement

This is not a new activity, but it is still a good one! Sometimes we forget about these activities from our own childhood, and it is so simple to create. My twins didn't know what hopscotch was until I drew it out and showed them how it worked. Often, we assume that kids know all the fun, yet old, play activities, but they don't unless someone has shown them. My children loved it and after I drew the one shown, they played with it for about 20 minutes, first trying to do it with both feet which they mastered in the first few minutes. Then they tried to do the hopscotch while hopping on one foot, jumping on one foot the entire time to successfully jump from numbers one through ten. If they fell or missed a number, they had to start over. In the beginning they couldn't even get to number four without falling. After practicing, within fifteen minutes they had mastered it and were able to hop through all the numbers without falling. It is a great gross motor skill-developing activity that also uses their balancing skills.

They can put their own imagination and creative skills into practice by creating their very own hopscotch. My kids had no problem jumping in and creating their own. They made about a dozen of them in over an hour. They made some with circles, some with gaps, and some that had numbers out of order. I loved seeing their creativity at work! There aren't any hard and fast rules about hopscotch. They can make them up as they go along. However, they can't get started unless someone shows them how to create a hopscotch with some basic rules (which of course they are welcome to change as they create their own hopscotch).

31 Chalk Obstacle Course

Supplies Needed

☐ pavement with plenty of space

☐ a stopwatch (or phone with this feature)

☐ Chalk

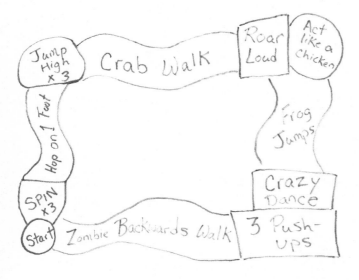

This activity was a winner in our household! When I put my five-year-old son Charlie to bed that night he said he had the most fun ever! That is high praise coming from a five-year-old especially when all it took was some chalk and a few minutes of my time to create the course.

I created the course by drawing boxes and shapes that connected to one another. You can see the example in the photo and the drawing that I made as a suggestion to help you create your own. Simply write a different physical activity within each shape. It took me about ten minutes to draw the course on the pavement in our driveway courtyard. If you don't have a large space, you can always draw your course straight down a sidewalk. Do whatever will work for the pavement space that you have.

Below are some suggestions for movements that you can put in each space. Some require more space, so keep that in mind when you are drawing the activity on the pavement. For example, frog jumps need more space than spinning in a circle.

- Pushups
- Crab walk
- Jump as high as you can
- Crazy dance
- Touch your toes
- Roar
- Pretend you are an elephant

- Meow like a kitty
- Bark like a dog
- Frog hops
- Bunny hops
- Spin
- Twirl
- Snap

- Clap your hands
- Whistle a song
- Hop
- Touch your head and your toes
- Walk backwards
- Jumping jacks

Once you have created your chalk obstacle course, it's time for the kids to try it out. You will have to read them out loud to the kids if they are unable to read. For my twins, who cannot fully read yet, they followed their older sister who could read, so they copied what she did. After they completed the course a few times they began to remember what to do in each shape or space. We then played a simple game to see who could do the course the fastest. I used the stopwatch on my phone. The first time they each did the course it took them well over a minute and a half. After they did the course several times using the stopwatch, they all were quite fast and completed it in under a minute. I timed each child separately, so they wouldn't rush one another or run into each other.

This activity helps with developing gross motor skills, coordination, balance, speed, and agility. It is also a great way to burn up their energy and get their wiggles out. It is definitely great for getting them some exercise. My kids are very active and full of energy from morning until evening. This activity was a perfect one for them, which is probably why Charlie said it was the best day ever!

32 Nature Scavenger Hunt

Supplies Needed

☐ Scavenger hunt printable and the great outdoors

Fall Scavenger Hunt

Flower	Pumpkin	Yellow Leaf
Pinecone	Bird	Orange Leaf
Acorn	Twig	Smooth Rock
Animal Footprints	Animal	Rough Rock

One November a couple of years ago I created a nature scavenger hunt. We were staying at a campground with another family who had kids the same age. We couldn't swim since it was too cold outside, so I came up with some fun activities for the kids to do while we were at the campsite. I printed the scavenger hunt sheets and had them on hand before we even left our house for the trip. I was prepared to make it a fun time even if it was cold outside!

The kids enjoyed the nature hunt. I had a prize basket filled with small toys. For every child that completed their nature hunt they got to pick a prize from the basket. Some of the parents went with the kids on a long walk to complete the nature hunt activity.

Doing a nature activity makes children much more aware of their natural surroundings. When they are looking for specific parts of nature, they end up seeing more than they would have had they not had such an activity.

This activity gets them outside, active, and involved with nature. They also use their observation and searching skills, which come in handy because they will likely be looking for their shoes for the next ten years. Any activity that can help them develop better searching and hunting skills is a good thing!

This is a sensory activity, especially if you ask them to collect items from nature, such as the pinecone, smooth rock, rough rock, acorn, leaves, and twigs. This nature-driven activity helps children make discoveries on their own. You will be amazed how excited they get when they are the first to find something on the list. This is a fun activity, but one that greatly boosts their observation skills.

You can find the printable shown on my website. Use the search terms "scavenger hunt" in the search bar of www.livingjoydaily.com. You can also use the web address below for the exact location of the printable: http://livingjoydaily.com/2017/11/13/free-thanksgiving-activities-for-kids.

33 DIY Cardstock Puzzle Play

Supplies Needed   ☐ Cardstock paper   ☐ markers or crayons   ☐ scissors

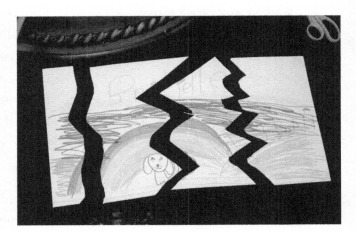

For this project I gave my kids cardboard paper for them to draw a picture. We have utilized cardstock in the past and it worked well, too. This particular cardboard paper is from our drycleaner. My husband's shirts are folded onto these cardboard sheets when his shirts are cleaned at the dry cleaners. We save the pieces of cardboard from the shirts and use them for various art and craft activities. They happened to be quite useful for this project, but card stock paper also works just fine.

After you have each child create their work of art, you then flip it over and draw lines for cutting the artwork into pieces. We did pieces that made the puzzles look more like sequencing puzzles, as you can see in the photo. You can draw the lines for the puzzle however you like.

Once the lines are drawn, I let the kids cut on the lines. They got to make their very own puzzles! This activity helps with developing hand strength and scissor-cutting skills, especially since this paper is a little thicker than normal paper. They also got to use their imagination and draw whatever they wanted for the puzzle. Their fine motor skills were used for drawing, cutting, and putting the puzzle back together.

This activity does require scissors. Only allow your children to use safety scissors for this activity or any activity for that matter. Adult supervision is required for this activity. Do not allow children who cannot safely use safety scissors to do the cutting. Do the cutting for them if they cannot be safe with scissors.

34 Snowflakes

Supplies Needed

☐ Paper and scissors

This activity is an easy crowd pleaser! If children can use scissors, then they are ready for this activity. This activity will help with their hand strength, scissor cutting skills, and fine motor skills. Because the paper is folded, it is more difficult to cut through the layers. I had to give my kids a bit of encouragement, telling them they could cut through the layers if they focused and tried hard enough. They did it! It is a good way to build up their hand strength. They got to be creative with this project too. They were excited to unfold each snowflake after they finished cutting.

My daughter was able to correctly fold after I demonstrated the process for her. My five-year-old twins needed some assistance with the folding. You can see in the photo how to fold. Once you have it in a square, you need to cut the excess paper from the bottom. Rectangular snowflakes don't look quite right. Make sure that they don't cut off any of the edges completely that are holding the sections of the folded snowflake together. My kids learned this lesson through trial and error and yours will too. When they open their snowflake and it falls apart, you know that they cut the edges off completely, which then divides the snowflake into pieces.

An easy way to get started is to draw some triangle and half-moon shapes along each edge and corner of the folded paper. Have the child cut on these lines. This will ensure that they don't cut off an entire edge that holds the snowflake together.

This was a good lesson for planning and cause-and-effect, as I discussed with my children why their snowflakes fell apart. We refolded one that was already cut out, so we could talk about where to cut and where not to cut, and my kids were able to clearly see that completely cutting off one side would make it fall apart. This is a good project that boosts their creativity, and they also learn in the process.

This activity is also a great way to decorate the ceilings in a classroom, playroom, or bedroom. Use a hole punch to create a hole at the top of each snowflake. Tie each snowflake onto a string and hang from the ceiling. You can also tape them to the windows. It makes the space feel more festive and fun!

This cutting activity requires the use of scissors. As I stated previously, only allow children to use safety scissors for any type of cutting activity, and even then, adult supervision is required. Do the cutting for them if they cannot use scissors safely.

35 Tea Party

Supplies Needed   ☐ Tea party set and food items if desired

 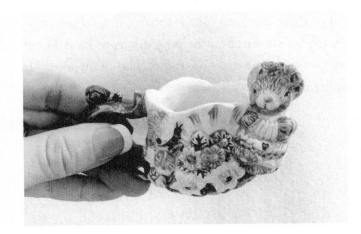

The goal for this activity is to use it as an opportunity to talk about manners. It is also a fun activity that most children enjoy doing. They like to pretend being prim and proper, sticking out their pinky while sipping their tea. My daughter is always reminding her brothers not to slurp their tea (which is usually lemonade). I always bring out some crackers and cloth napkins when we play teatime. That way we can talk about how to place the napkin in their lap and practice our eating manners such as closing our mouth while we eat.

Below is a list of the manners that you can teach your child, as you have your tea party:

- Guests should stand behind their chairs and they can be seated when the host pulls out his or her chair to be seated (this helps teach patience)

- The host pours her guests their tea

- Take only small, careful sips of the tea

- Always say please and thank you

- Napkins should be spread in their lap

- Food should be passed around the table

- No reaching for food plates

- If someone wants a dish or plate of food, they must ask for it to be passed, and must ask using the words please and thank you

- No belching or other bodily noises

- Excuse me is said if something embarrassing does happen

- Mouths should be closed when chewing and eating

- Stir tea without clinking on the inside of the cup

- Set down teacup gently after drinking, so there is little or no noise

All of these manners can be taught at a simple play tea party. It is a good way to help them better understand that manners are about helping others to have an enjoyable dining experience. Feel free to take the opportunity to have everyone dress up and perhaps wear some fancy hats too. It will help everyone feel like it is a festive and authentic tea party experience.

36 Moon Sand

☐ Flour   ☐ baby oil   ☐ a container for the moon sand

This is a great recipe for simple moon sand. This turns flour into a material that feels like moldable sand that you would find on sugary sand beaches in places like South Florida. It is so simple to make as only two ingredients are needed. It is an inexpensive activity and easy activity. If you keep the moon sand sealed in a container for playtime it should stay clean and usable for quite some time. Our last batch I kept for a full month before tossing out and it was still working and looking just fine.

Ingredients:

- 8 cups of all-purpose flour
- 1 cup baby oil

Once you combine the ingredients spend about five minutes mixing it with your hands so that the oil blends well and is evenly distributed throughout the flour. This is a sensory activity that you can get your kids to do too! They should enjoy the feeling of the moon sand as it begins to take shape. It is a great way to get them involved in the process of making the moon sand and you can keep your hands clean. Once it is fully mixed you can see that it can be made into shapes and is moldable like fresh snow or fine beach sand. As they build with the moon sand they are using their construction skills, planning skills, and fine motor skills.

37 Beach Play with Moon Sand

Supplies Needed

- ☐ Moon sand
- ☐ rakes
- ☐ seashells (if you have them)
- ☐ beach toys such as shovels
- ☐ sandcastle molds

This is a great way to play with moon sand. Let your children pretend that they are playing with sand at the beach! The more moon sand you have the better. Two batches of moon sand can nicely fill an under the bed plastic storage bin, which is the perfect depth and size for this kind of activity. We have a single batch as shown in the photo and used a 16-quart storage bin for the sand. It worked well, but later we doubled the batch and put it in a larger rectangle bin (one of those under-the-bed storage containers I mentioned). This allowed all three of my kids to play at the same time. I got tired of the fighting over this particular activity, so we solved that problem by making a double batch.

If you don't have any sand toys a great place to pick them up cheap is at a retail discount store like the Dollar Tree or Dollar General. We had shells on hand from previous beach vacations. If you don't have any in your home, you can pick up a bag of beautiful, real shells from Walmart. They're not expensive and can be found in the craft section. Kids love playing with the shells in the moon sand. When you are done with the sand and want to keep the shells for another activity, simply rinse them with dish soap and water.

Playing with moon sand has the same developmental benefits as that of playing in real sand since children are still using their fine motor skills. They also develop their hand-eye coordination as they work to build, mold, and create with the sand. This activity also helps their creativity and imagination blossom as they think of different objects, shapes, and patterns to make in the sand.

38 Mini Canvas Artwork

☐ Mini canvases   ☐ washable paints   ☐ paint brushes

We purchased mini canvases, which typically come in packs of twos and threes at the Dollar Tree, depending on size. You can find small canvases at Hobby Lobby and Michaels too, but they will cost slightly more. The washable paint set we used is from Walmart. My kids are always wanting to create "real art." This means that they want to paint on canvases or watercolor paper. They like to create artwork that they can display in our playroom or give to friends. This is an awesome project that keeps them busy and they tend to concentrate more on their work, since I emphasize that they are using "real" art supplies. It is a fun way to create works of art for grandparents, aunts, uncles, and teachers. The small canvases are just the right size for gifts.

The washable paints are very useful. Acrylic is another option, but if they get acrylic paint on their clothing it will not wash out. Acrylic will stain clothing. Therefore, my "go-to "for painting projects like these are washable, non-toxic, poster paints. They are inexpensive and can be purchased in packs of ten or twenty colors.

Make sure that you have paintbrushes in a variety of sizes. Wide paintbrushes are useful when kids want a lot of coverage, such as painting the entire background one color. Smaller brushes are needed when they want to paint details. You can find variety packs of paintbrushes at craft stores or in the crafting section at Walmart or Target. Your children do not need expensive paint brushes, but a variety of sizes is helpful as it allows them to experiment with the different brushes and use their creativity.

Painting is a very helpful activity in developing fine motor skills. It is also an opportunity for children to use their imagination and creativity. You can use the painting session as an opportunity to talk about different colors and ask the child to identify the colors as they paint. If they are slightly older, you can discuss mixing colorings and what colors result from the mixing of which color combinations. Art is a great way to play and learn at the same time.

39 Chalk Road Course

☐ Chalk and pavement

This is a great outside activity that gets your kids active and moving. Drawing out some roadways in your driveway, sidewalk, and/or courtyard can be done in about ten minutes. It is good exercise for you too if you participate in the drawing of the roads.

If bending over to draw these roads isn't for you, there is a handy tool on Amazon called the "Walking Chalk Stand Up Sidewalk Chalk Holder." This tool is amazing and ingenious! It allows you to stand up and write with the chalk. Imagine holding a broom handle, but at the end you have chalk. Yes, that is a smart, easy, and efficient way to do chalk writing with your kids. I can afford the $11 for the chalk holder for the sake of my back, so from here forward I am going that route as I just purchased one online for myself. I have spent enough hours of my life hunched over drawing with chalk on the ground. Once again, I am not being paid by anyone to promote their products. I just like to share with readers the helpful gadgets and toys that have worked for our family. I am not getting paid or compensated by anyone for using or promoting their products.

Back to our actual activity—the road course! This is a simple activity that your kids will delight in doing! Draw out some roadways with chalk on your pavement. I like to create a large loop and then usually a road that cuts through the middle of the looping roadway. This way I can direct all traffic in one direction around the loop, which makes it a bit safer. The kids will spend hours on their road course using their bikes, trikes, skates, scooters, and more.

The two ride-on toys in the photo for this activity are crowd pleasers! I am especially a fan of the little one on the left called a "Scuttlebug trike." This little ride-on toy collapses so it is easy to transport. It can even be folded up and carried in a suitcase, it gets that compact. The nice thing about this small ride-on toy is that it is just the right size for use in the house during the winter. My twins would loop around our kitchen and living room area, which connects with a hallway to the rest of the home. This little loop would keep them entertained and allow them to burn off their energy when it was too cold to play outside. The wheels were soft enough that when they ran into any walls it never caused any major damage, maybe a scuff or two, but nothing that a magic eraser couldn't fix. All three of my kids loved the two Scuttlebugs we owned. They were the favorite ride-on toy for all three of my kids as toddlers and older.

The ride-on toy on the right in the photo is a plasma car. This was a gift from family, and it was also a favorite for many years. Forget regular trikes. Those are boring compared to the plasma car and Scuttlebugs. The plasma car uses twisting, turning, and wiggle movement to move forward. Both of these ride-on toys help kids develop gross motor skills and balancing skills. They also learn to play cooperatively as they create roadways and follow some basic rules, such as no running into other riders, and you must go one way around the circle. Following rules is an important skill to learn as they prepare for school. Having play activities such as this one can be helpful in developing their ability to follow instructions and abide by rules.

Now that my kids have graduated beyond Scuttlebugs, trikes, and plasma cars it is all about riding bikes and scooters. The chalk road courses are still great for bikes and scooters too! In our home we are firm with the rules. If they run into one another with their bikes, then playtime ends, and the bikes go back into the garage. Safety is first. My boys tend to want to create crashes. Accidents happen, but in our home, many can be avoided simply by following the rules, which includes no causing accidents and crashes on purpose.

40 Chalk Town

☐ Chalk and pavement space

This activity is much like creating the roadways using chalk, but in this case, you are adding another dimension of creative play by using shapes that represent buildings. For this activity we drew squares or rectangles around the perimeter of the roadways as well as some in the center. Ask your children what kind of buildings and locations are needed for their town. Some that we typically include in ours are a post office, gym, homes, park, restaurant, emergency room, and stores. You can then incorporate activities into these different locations. For example, you can set up the post office using the instructions from activity #70 in this book. You can also incorporate activity #86, which is the "move it sticks" activity. These sticks can be placed in the gym space. Every time that they ride past the gym they must stop and select at least one move it stick and do the activity before hopping back on their bike or scooter. The goal is to create imaginative play and activities that keep their minds and bodies moving while they are having fun.

Another activity to incorporate into your chalk town is #92, which is restaurant play. You can have the kids bring out some kitchen play items that would help to create a restaurant atmosphere. If you have child-size table and chairs, you could bring those out and put them in the play space, too.

Activity #62 is creating a pretend grocery store. This is another activity that would be fun to incorporate into your chalk town. It doesn't require much to get their imagination going. Even a few items for sale, with a makeshift register is all you need to represent the grocery store and get them playing.

Typically, I help the kids draw their chalk towns. It is a bit of work and for children under the age of seven it may be asking them too much to do it on their own. You can help them draw but ask them to get involved in the process. My daughter created parking spaces next to the businesses I drew around our chalk town. That way everyone knew where their scooter or bike was to be parked when they stopped at each location.

Once the chalk town is drawn, they can play on their own, or you can join in if you would like. I will play with my kids for about ten minutes, which gets them very excited about the activity. Then I leave them to play on their own. My children can play for over an hour quite contentedly with this particular activity.

This play activity incorporates role play and imaginative play. They are also using their gross motor skills. They will likely set up some rules for their town as well as how to play. For example, my kids were required to use Brielle's parking spaces, and they couldn't put their bikes or ride on toys anywhere else in the driveway space. This cooperative play helps children learn how to work with one another and to set their own play rules. You can set an example by setting a few initial rules, such as traffic goes one way around the circle and no running into one another on purpose. Then you can ask them what other rules their town should have. This can open the door for some organizational thought processes and planning skills. Both are great skills to work on developing in early childhood.

The idea is to have fun, not make it work, so don't make this overly complicated. If you spend more time setting it up than the kids actually play, you are probably doing far too much. I spent about 10 minutes drawing the town and then another 10 minutes playing with them and talking about their town rules and how it functions. They went on to play for over an hour on their own. They had a great time as they always do with this activity!

41 Slime Play

- ☐ 4 ounces of white craft glue (this is one regular-size container of Elmer's or similar brand of white glue)
- ☐ 6-8 teaspoons of liquid starch
- ☐ 3 teaspoons of water
- ☐ a bowl
- ☐ food coloring (if you want to add color)

This is a recipe to make slime. It is not difficult to make. When you make it at home, you can ensure that it isn't overly sticky. We have purchased slime, and it has been so sticky we couldn't get it off our hands without major hand washing, not to mention that it stuck to fabric and didn't come out of clothing until it was machine washed. When you make it at home you can add more starch to reduce and eliminate the stickiness. You want the slime to be flexible and stretchy for play and manipulation, but you don't want it to stick to your hands more than it sticks to itself.

To make the slime you first mix the water and the glue together. If you are going to add food coloring do it now before you add any starch to the mix. Once it is completely combined you can add the liquid starch one teaspoon at a time. Thoroughly mix each teaspoon of starch into the glue mixture before you add any more starch. When it begins to form a ball, you'll know the slime is becoming the right consistency. Because glues and starches differ, you may need to add more starch or more glue. You will need to add more starch if it is overly sticky. If you add too much starch that the slime begins to break into chunks, then add some more glue. It can be a bit of an experiment when making slime. Make sure that you have extra glue and starch on hand to add if needed.

I let my kids do all the mixing. They initially mix with a spoon. Once it becomes firm enough that it is forming a ball, they can then begin kneading it with their hands and remove the ball from the bowl. They can keep kneading it for a minute or two and it should be ready for play.

Slime play is a sensory activity that engages their fine motor skills. They are also using their creativity and imagination while playing with the slime. My daughter was creating stingrays and then spider webs with her slime. It is neat to see what they create and think to do with the slime. Just don't let them get it in their hair. You will regret that decision and so will they.

42 Foam Slime Play

☐ The recipe from the previous page (make it a double batch)
☐ a package of foam balls from the craft section that are made for slime play

Helping participate in this recipe involves great sensory play for kids. They can start by using their hands to mix the package of balls into the slime. My kids loved the feeling of mixing these foam balls into the slime. We did have to add a little more glue, and then it was too much glue, so we added a little more starch. Again, it takes a bit of experimenting to get the right consistency with each batch. Think of the recipe, as general guidelines, but use your best judgement to get the correct consistency.

The foam balls were purchased at Walmart for under $2 a package. You must double the recipe from the previous activity (#41) in order to make enough slime to use the entire package of foam balls. They now carry these foam balls at the Dollar Tree in a variety of colors. They can be found in the crafting aisle.

This activity is great for fine motor skill development, creating a sensory touching experience that is unique, and it also allows them to use their imagination to create with the slime.

Make sure to store it in a Ziploc bag when they are done playing with the slime. That way it can be used and played with again.

Here are some helpful tips on removing slime if it gets into the carpet. Remove as much of the slime with your fingers as you can. Then add vinegar and water to a spray bottle. The mixture should be two parts vinegar to one-part water. Before applying to the carpet, test first in an inconspicuous spot to ensure that it is safe to use on your carpet. If you feel that it is ok to use on your carpet, spray the slime and saturate the spot. You should see it begin to dissolve. Blot with a paper towel removing as much of the slime and mixture as you can. Repeat the spraying and blotting until it is completely gone.

43 Bubble Play

Supplies Needed

☐ Bubble solution   ☐ various bubble wands   ☐ a tray for dipping the wands

Bubbles and chalk are two of the staples of childhood play. Bubble wands are a good investment that don't cost a great deal and can be used and re-used for years. We have an outdoor cabinet in our patio area with various play items as well as our chicken supplies. There is one bin dedicated to bubble play supplies. This bin contains a variety of large and small bubble wands along with the trays for dipping. My kids could play with bubbles every day. It is a simple play activity that brings great joy to both children and adults.

Once you get your kids some amazing wands you will never go back to the simple bubble containers that you get from the store. You can also make your own bubble solution, making it easier to keep up with the bubble play and not have to run to the store every time that they run out. Here is our bubble recipe that works well for these wands and creates hours of fun!

Bubble Recipe:

- 6 cups of warm water
- 1 cup of dish soap (Dawn works best in my experience)
- ¼ cup of corn syrup (I use Karo)

As you add the soap to the water do it very gently so that it doesn't foam up or develop too many bubbles. You don't want to use up the bubbles before the kids get to play! Stir very gently and then allow it to sit for about a ½ hour before use. You can make batches of this solution and store it in a used detergent container. The kind that sit on the countertop and have a spigot are especially useful. Using one of those countertop containers filled with bubble solution allows you to create your very own bubble refill station.

You can find various bubble wand kits online. I spent less than $15 on our wand kit and it came with over 20 pieces in a variety of sizes. Make sure to put them away when finished so that you have them for many months and years to come.

Bubble play helps ignite a child's imagination. It also builds their confidence as they improve their ability to make nice, big bubbles. My kids get so excited when they create perfect bubbles that float high up in the sky and will shout in excitement for me to look at their creations.

44 Giant Bubbles

Supplies Needed

☐ Bubble solution for giant bubbles ☐ a bucket ☐ giant bubble-making wands

Making giant bubbles is a great deal of fun for kids and it also is a great use of their motor skills. It is not as easy to make giant bubbles as it is to make regular-size bubbles with plastic wands. There is some skill involved, but children can be directed on how to make these bubbles successfully. Some tips you can provide to your child include the following:

• Make sure that the bubble wand is untangled. It can still make bubbles with a tangle or two, but it works much more effectively if there aren't any tangles in the strings.

• When dipping the wand into the solution, have the wand closed, so that the strings can dip in all together at once.

• When pulling the wand strings out of the solution allow it to drip into the bucket for a few seconds, so that bubble solution isn't wasted.

• Open the wand so that a circle-like opening is created with the strings.

• Walk smoothly at a slow to medium pace so that air goes in and creates a bubble.

• Close the wands together to close off the bubble. If the wands are not closed, lasting bubbles cannot be created. To create bubbles that float away, the wands must be brought together and closed to close the end of the bubble. Otherwise, long bubbles will be created, but they will not last, and they will not be able to float away from the wand.

This activity will help children improve their hand-eye coordination. It also helps them with planning and timing skills. It is a fun activity that they will enjoy doing, and they won't even realize that they are learning and developing skills in the process. Be patient in this activity, as it is a skill development. Making giant bubbles requires time, concentration, focus, and effort. Encourage them to keep trying and go over the tips above with them if they are having difficulty.

As for bubble solution here is what we have used that has proven successful (you can find a wide variety of suggestions online, but this has worked for us):

- 12 cups of warm water
- 1 cup of Dawn dish soap
- 1 cup of corn starch
- 2 tbsp of baking powder (not to be confused with baking soda)
- 2 tbsp of Glycerin (which you can find on Amazon or at craft stores)

First, you need to dissolve the corn starch in the water. Stir until it is mostly dissolved. It is difficult to get all the corn starch to dissolve but try to dissolve as much as possible. Next, add the rest of the ingredients but add them gently so that you don't create foaming action or bubbles on the surface. Allow this mixture to sit for at least an hour before using. I have allowed it to sit overnight, and it seems to work even better. Stir occasionally if you see any corn starch on the bottom.

Another option for making solution for giant bubbles is to purchase a product called "BUBBLE THING Big Bubble Mix." You can find this product on Amazon. This solution is mixed with water and dish soap. It is not a cheap product, but it works the best of all bubble solutions we have tried to make at home.

Giant bubble wands used to be more difficult to find. These days you can go online and find everything just a click away. Amazon has a wide variety of vendors that sell giant bubble wands. I suggest that you read reviews so you can find wands that others have had success in using. Use the phrase "giant bubble wands" to search and you should find plenty of wands for sale. You can now find three and four packs of these wands for under $20 (of course there is no guarantee on these prices in the future). These wands are awesome for creating lots of fun and memories with friends! It is a great activity to do for a playdate with another family.

Here are some additional tips for giant bubble making. Bubbles work best in humid or muggy weather. Find a shady spot if you can for your bubble-making experience. Bubbles last longer and are easier to make if they are not in direct sunlight. You can still make them in the direct sun, but you will have greater success on humid days where you don't have direct sunlight on your bubble-making area.

45 Outdoor Obstacle Course

Supplies Needed

- ☐ Pool noodles
- ☐ orange cones
- ☐ hula hoops
- ☐ a ball
- ☐ a bucket
- ☐ spot markers if you have them

In recent years my kids have become obsessed with obstacle courses. They create their own and sometimes I help them create more elaborate and sophisticated courses. The photo shows one of the courses I recently made with them. It took about 20 minutes to set up. We probably spent more time finding the items in the house than we spent setting it all up.

First, we staked small pool noodles into the ground, which they had to army crawl under. This was just the start for their gross motor skill activities in this course. Then we placed hula hoops on the lawn. They had to hop from the center of one hoop to the next. After the hula hoops, they needed to zigzag run around the orange cones. At the end of the cones was a spot marker. They had to stand on that marker and throw a ball into a bucket. The bucket was six to eight feet away from the spot. They had to keep trying until they got the ball into the bucket. This helped them practice their hand-eye coordination. Once they got it into the bucket, they next walked across two pool noodles, balance beam style. This required some balancing skills. Finally, they got to the dot markers, which were set up in a hopscotch pattern. Once they completed the hopscotch, they were done!

The first time they did it for fun, so they could see how everything worked. Then they each took a turn completing the course while being timed. I simply pulled up the stopwatch feature on my phone. While we were watching whoever was doing the course, we cheered for that person. They weren't competing against one another's scores. Instead they were trying to create and beat their own personal records. They did the course many, many times, each time beating their previous score. When they began, they completed the course in approximately two minutes. After many times going through the course being timed, they were all in the thirty-second range.

This activity helped sharpen their gross motor skills, and they developed greater speed using those skills. Obstacle courses are fun for kids, and this activity gets them physically active. This kind of exercise is great at helping combat childhood obesity. They don't even realize that they are exercising, especially when they are running the course repeatedly for over an hour trying to improve their course time!

This activity is great exercise combined with motor skill development. It is also an opportunity for them to use their creative skills. They can modify the course or add their own ideas. My kids added the slide and climbing wall on their playset to the course once they felt that they had reached their ultimate low scores on the first course. They modified the course and kept finding new ways to make their obstacle course more interesting. It kept them busy for hours while their creative skills were put to work. They were active that entire afternoon thanks to some hula hoops and pool noodles from the Dollar Tree. We already had the other items on hand. Play doesn't have to be expensive to be beneficial both physically and mentally.

46 Bristle Blocks

☐ A set of Bristle Blocks

Bristle Blocks are plastic textured building blocks that lock together via the bristles on each block. The texture of the blocks makes this a real sensory play activity. Playing with Bristle blocks is helpful for a young child's development, including hand-eye coordination, construction skills, and imaginative building skills.

These blocks are intended for toddlers and young children. The blocks have soft interlocking bristles, so they are great for young children who are just learning to build things. This toy helps with hand and finger muscles as it can require some effort to put the bristles together and then pull them apart. The blocks can go together on a variety of angles, so this makes the playtime and building even more creative. Fine motor development occurs as children play with these blocks and manipulate the pieces together for building creations that they think up and design.

47 Slip-n-Slide Fun

Supplies Needed
☐ A Slip-n-Slide   ☐ water source   ☐ hose for hook up

Slip-n-Slides are not a new way to play. However, they don't seem to be as popular in recent years. Perhaps it's because toys go in cycles of use, and people have forgotten this old, but very fun way for kids to play. This is an excellent gross motor skill activity, as they run, jump and slide on their stomach, all while timing it out just right. They won't get their timing and jumping right the first or even second time. It takes some practice, and it is indeed a skill. Some kids take longer to learn, but if they keep practicing, they can figure it out and their depth perception skills will also improve. Depth perception tends to be the biggest issue for children using the Slip-n-Slide. They jump onto their stomach too soon or too late because they misjudge the distance as they are running, which means their depth perception and spatial perception skills need some work. This activity helps with visual and spatial development, and they get firsthand experience in fine tuning their depth perception skills.

This is a perfect way to get kids outside, and they also get great exercise from this activity. If it is a hot summer day and kids don't want to be outside because it is too hot, but they are bored inside, then set up a Slip-n-Slide and you will have them entertained for hours if not the entire day. We set this one up (shown in the photo) for three days while on a camping trip. It was used for hours on end each day by our own three kids and by many other children at the campground who asked if they could join in on the fun. We set basic rules, such as taking turns and no turning off the water while the Slip-n-Slide is in use. Once they slid to the end, they needed to get off quickly, so the next person had their turn. The next person could only begin running when the last person was completely off the Slip-n-Slide. Children who break these rules tend to get hurt; we know this from personal experience.

This Slip-n-Slide hooked up to a hose and had sprinkler action, making it lots of fun. This activity is great for toddlers through teens. They all seem to enjoy the Slip-n-Slide. It's a wonderful experience and promotes use of their gross motor skills.

Small children can drown in even an inch of water, so adult supervision is required at all times once a Slip-n-Slide is set up. Read the instructions and warnings that come with the product when purchasing a Slip-n-Slide.

In warmer seasons, you can find Slip-n-Slides at stores such as Walmart and Target. They can also be found on Amazon year-round.

48 Lima Bean Alphabet Sort and Match

Supplies Needed

- ☐ Dried lima beans
- ☐ 2 ice cube trays
- ☐ a fine point Sharpie marker
- ☐ a regular Sharpie marker

For this activity, you will need 2 ice cube trays. We were able to pick up a two-pack at the local Dollar Tree, and we purchased a package of dried lima beans at the grocery store. We used two kinds of Sharpie markers for this project. The fine point type is for writing the letters of the alphabet on the lima beans. The regular Sharpie is for writing the alphabet inside the ice cube trays, as you can see in the photos. My seven-year-old daughter drew the letters of the alphabet on the lima beans. She liked this activity so much that she made two sets when we only needed one! She wrote the letters on both sides of each lima bean to make them easier for children to identify the letters.

This is a sorting and matching game. Provide the empty ice cube trays to a preschooler and then a bowl with lima beans that have the letters of the alphabet written on them. Their goal is to match the lima bean letters with the letters in the ice cube trays and place them in the correct ice cube slots.

This activity helps with letter recognition. It is also an activity that works on developing their fine motor skills. If this is easy enough for your preschool aged children, then you can pull up the stopwatch on your phone and time them. Time them once putting all the alphabet letters into the correct ice cube slots. Their goal for the next time is to beat that last score. This activity will help with their cognitive speed and ability to use their fine motor skills quickly, while thinking fast. It is a mental agility, fine motor agility task.

49 Brain Flakes

☐ A set of brain flakes or creative flakes

This manipulative is another one that we discovered at our preschool. My son Alex become transfixed by this activity. We had to purchase a set for our own home after they finished preschool this school year. These lightweight flakes lock and link together to produce 3D creations. Children can use their imagination to create whatever they desire using these brain flakes. In the photo for this activity my daughter said that she created a large spaceship with smaller spaceship pods.

This toy is great for early childhood development. It is recommended for children ages three and up since the pieces are small. In using these brain flakes or creative flakes children learn to think independently as they create objects that they conjure up themselves. This toy is labeled as a STEM activity, which means that it involves the learning of **s**cience, **t**echnology, **e**ngineering, and **m**ath while children are playing with this toy. It is a highly educational toy that engages children in imaginative play that utilizes STEM concepts.

You can find this product on Amazon or online by searching both brain flakes and creative flakes. They are made by a variety of manufacturers. Read the reviews and find the set that works best for your children.

50 Jenga Blocks for Building

Supplies Needed

☐ A set of Jenga Blocks

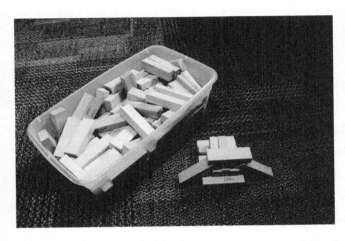

We have Jenga Blocks, but we haven't played Jenga much over the years. We purchased our Jenga set before we even had children. Now that the kids have discovered it, we found that our Jenga game makes for perfect building blocks. We have spent far more hours using the blocks for play, than actually playing a game of Jenga.

I have a humorous story about these blocks. My kids love them so much that we brought them on a camping trip with us, so the kids could play with them. One evening the adults were sitting around chatting while the kids were playing together on the floor of our camper. The grandmother of the other family's children noticed that her grandkids loved these blocks and she wanted to know where she could buy them for all of her grandkids. I said that they were "Jenga Blocks" and assumed that she knew what that meant. She obviously didn't, as she responded with, "do they come from a specialty toy shop because they look like really nice blocks, or can I find them at other stores like Target?" I had to explain that they came from our adult game, but they had been relinquished to the kids since they seemed to get more use of them than we did.

Our preschool classroom from this past school year also had a set in their classroom. Once again, not for actually playing Jenga, but instead for the kids to use as building blocks.

Keep your eye out for used sets at garage sales, estate sales, and thrift shops. The more blocks the better! People often sell their sets or give them away after they lose a few of the pieces. They may not want to play Jenga with them anymore, but they still make for very useful, well made, building blocks.

Building with blocks puts a child's construction and engineering skills into practice. They also use visual perception skills when they build with blocks. Many occupational therapists use blocks to treat children who need help developing fine motor skills. You can help your own children develop their fine motor skills by providing them with blocks for play time.

51 Pretend Cooking

Supplies Needed

☐ A play kitchen set
☐ children's play food items

☐ pots
☐ pan
☐ dishes

We purchased a Kidkraft kitchen set for our kids five years ago. They are still playing with the set almost daily. Our set is a staple in our playroom. Children, including mine, love to pretend to cook.

The kitchen set shown is from our preschool. It too gets lots of play and use! I like the one at the preschool better than our own since theirs is made of solid wood. Our Kidkraft set works well for home use, but probably wouldn't endure the wear and tear of constant use at a preschool like a set made from wood. If I could go back and purchase again, I would likely buy something similar to this wood set shown in the photo. I had no idea my kids would play with ours for so many years and how often they would use it.

It isn't too difficult to find a used kitchen play set if you can't afford to purchase a new one. You can find plastic food items, the play dishes, etc. at the Dollar Tree, Walmart, Target, Amazon and many other stores. It is a popular toy item, so you can find these accessory play items almost anywhere that toys are sold.

Playing with a play kitchen helps children with social development. The play kitchen is usually a place where children like to gather to play and interact. This type of play activity facilitates teamwork, teaches sharing, and encourages both role play and imaginative play. Children also learn about valuable life skills like organization, order, and follow-through when playing in a play kitchen.

52 Lacing and Tying

☐ Melissa and Doug Lacing Shoe

This inexpensive Melissa and Doug lacing shoe is perfect for teaching children how to lace a shoe and how to tie the strings. The basic skill of tying one's own shoes usually develops around kindergarten and first grade age, but younger children enjoy practicing and learning how to lace. You can always give a child one of your tennis shoes and have them practice as well. The reason this Melissa and Doug lacing shoe works so well is because the shoe is made of wood, which makes it easier for a child to lace through this material. It also has holes that are just the right size for lacing, which is important to note since some shoes come with tiny holes that make the lacing process quite difficult.

As well as lacing and tying skills, this toy is also wonderful for developing fine motor skills. There are plenty of cute shoe tying videos on YouTube that you can play for your child. I was in my daughter's kindergarten classroom one day when the teacher played one of these videos. It was an adorable learning video, and the kids loved it! It helped my daughter as she was just learning to tie her shoes and she remembered some of the tips from the video when she was at home practicing.

53 Social LEGO Play

Supplies Needed

☐ A LEGO table that seats multiple children
☐ chairs
☐ LEGO bricks

Children and LEGO building go hand-in-hand. I have yet to meet a child that doesn't like to play with them. They all like to play to varying degrees of course. LEGO play can lend itself to be a solitary play activity, but that doesn't have to be the case. LEGO tables that seat more than one child are wonderful for facilitating social LEGO play. The table shown in the photo was taken at my twin's preschool. There were always three or more children playing at this table during free play time. They would often help each other create and build highly imaginative structures such as battleships, parking garages, and forts for battle. Ideas seemed endless with these kids as they played off one another's ideas. LEGO bricks are recommended for ages three and up, although some three-year-old children put things in their mouth. LEGO bricks are also a serious choking hazard. When I was volunteering one day at the preschool this past school year, I discovered one of the five-year-old girls with a small piece in her mouth. At first, I thought it was a piece of candy and then found out it was a LEGO once I got her to open her mouth! Always be sure that children know they should not put LEGO bricks in their mouth. If they make a habit of putting small things in their mouth, then LEGO bricks probably are not a good play activity for that child.

LEGO play is a great fine motor skill development activity. They are also helpful in strengthening hands and fingers as it takes some force to connect and disconnect them. For smaller children that are unable to click together small LEGO pieces, they can start out with the larger and slightly easier to use Duplo building blocks.

LEGO play helps children develop communication skills as they play with other children and interact to build things together. LEGO play also involves problem-solving and planning skills. When they build a structure and it doesn't work out as initially planned, they have to re-assess and problem-solve the situation to make their project work. This sort of thinking is defined as lateral thinking because they often must think in a creative and new way in order to make their LEGO project work when their original plans and thoughts didn't work out.

54 Dry Erase Cards

Supplies Needed

☐ Dry erase cards and dry erase markers

There are many different dry erase card sets for sale online. Whatever you want to teach your child, you can probably find dry erase cards to help you with their learning. The most basic cards involve letters, numbers, and shapes, which are helpful for children to practice writing. Most children enjoy writing with the dry erase cards and markers. The cards shown have fun ways of helping the children learn to write the letters. For example, the card with the J and U on it has the child write smiles to practice making the bottom shape of these letters.

This is a good travel activity. They can write in their laps with these cardboard cards and they don't take up much space in the car. It is a good way to break up a monotonous car ride and they are learning at the same time.

This activity helps children with their writing skills, number and letter identification, fine motor skills, and development of hand strength through writing practice. As they are writing the same letter several times on the cards, as shown in the photo, they are creating muscle memory for each letter that they write repeatedly. Creating muscle memory makes it increasingly easier for children to write these letters in the future.

55 Lincoln Logs

Supplies Needed

☐ A set of Lincoln Logs

I grew up playing with Lincoln Logs. I had completely forgotten about them until I came across them two years ago in a retro toy catalog. Seriously? Lincoln Logs are retro? Apparently, I am that old. They are an old toy, but you can buy them new on Amazon. Lincoln Logs are making a comeback because it is a great learning toy that is truly timeless. The notched wood pieces fit together just like old-fashioned log homes are built. It is a great way to teach children about construction methods. Someday when they come across a log home built in this manner, they will have an understanding and some comprehension of how it was constructed because they will have built it on a smaller scale themselves.

I appreciate the fact that Lincoln Logs are still made from real wood. It is important for children to handle natural products, since so much of what they handle today is plastic or metal. Wood is real. Wood is natural. Lincoln Logs are both real and natural. This kind of play helps them develop building skills, creative thought processes, hand-eye coordination, problem solving skills, and analytical thinking.

There are a variety of Lincoln Log sets for sale on Amazon and other sources, but I suggest buying one with enough pieces. There are some that come with just over 100 pieces and others that come with well over 300 pieces. I look at this product as an investment in their development whichever brand you decide to buy.

56 Magnet Blocks

☐ A set of magnet blocks

I have one friend with super smart kids. Yes, you know what I am talking about. That friend that has three children who are all geniuses, while I am trying to make sure my child doesn't pick their nose in public. All kids are different, and I am thankful for my children even if one of them does pick their nose in public.

This friend with the genius children always has great ideas about learning toys. I have been picking her brain and watching what she does with her children since my twins were babies. One toy she recommended when my twins were still toddlers were magnet blocks. She said, "They may be too young, but you never know." I purchased them for Christmas just after my twins turned two, and they have been my son Alex's favorite toy for three solid years. I purchased a second set of these blocks for Christmas the next year as well, so the kids had even more magnet blocks for playing and creating. These are such a family favorite that we can't even go camping for a weekend without bringing them along. Forget about video games. All my kids need are hundreds of magnet blocks and they are entertaining themselves and creating masterpieces they want to show me for hours on end.

There are lots of different magnet blocks for sale. Read reviews online to find the best match for your family. We like the Magna-Tiles brand for our family. We haven't had a single block broken yet, from either of the sets we purchased.

Magnet blocks help children learn shapes. They also build 3-D structures with these blocks which helps develop engineering skills. They use their fine motor skills through this creative play activity. Magnet blocks also help children develop self-control and focus. They must be patient and focused to put the blocks together without having them fall. Using these blocks while creating 3-D structures also builds basic geometry skills. These toys are a winner, and I am glad my genius friend, with her genius children, told me about them!

57 Linking

☐ Linking chains

This is a learning toy that doesn't take up much space and is very inexpensive. For under $10, we purchased a set of 200 links (there is no guarantee on future prices as they are always changing). Just use the term "linking chains" when searching for this learning activity online.

I witnessed my twins counting to 100 for the first time while playing with this toy. They were in their preschool classroom, and the children chained together 100 of these links. The chain was laid out across their main classroom on the floor. They counted with their teacher out loud as children added links to their long line of chained links. They were excited and cheered when they reached 100. It was fun to watch the kids get excited about counting to 100 and accomplishing this chain link together as a team.

This activity can help children learn about counting, patterns, sorting, and teamwork. They can also have fun making bracelets, necklaces, snakes, belts, and other items out of this toy. This is a fine motor activity that helps children with finger grasping and improves finger strength as they manipulate the links to string them together.

58 Number Matching Play with Rockets

Supplies Needed

☐ Felt
☐ fabric markers
☐ scissors
☐ fabric glue or hot glue

This is a matching activity. Children are provided with 20 rockets numbered 1-10. The first 10 are numbered with dots. The remaining 10 rockets are labeled numerically, as shown in the photo.

To make these yourself, you will need to purchase felt in a variety of colors. When you are creating the rockets make sure that your rockets match in color when they are the same value. For example, the rocket with nine dots is green, and the rocket with the number nine is also green. You will need orange and yellow felt for the flames at the end of the rockets. The body of the rockets can be 10 different colors if you would like. The rocket flames are the only part that need to be glued to the body of the rockets. The rest of the work is simply writing the numbers or dots. They are quite easy to make. Use a fabric marker to draw the dots and the numbers. This makes it easier than painting them on.

To cut out the rockets make a template using cardstock or a piece of cardboard. This will ensure that each of the rockets is the same.

This activity will help children with number recognition and development of their math skills. They learn about matching while using their fine motor skills.

There is no rule saying that you need to stick with the rocket theme. You can make boats, crowns, bumble bees, or whatever your child likes best. The goal is to get them playing and interested in doing a learning activity that is also fun.

59 Tree Wooden Block Imaginative Play

☐ Tree wooden blocks

These are authentic tree wooden blocks, which can be found on Amazon or made by someone who is handy. It is always wonderful to get children playing with authentic items from nature that are also safe for them. These pieces have been cut and then sanded so that your kids won't get splinters or slivers from the wood. You can find these on Amazon using the term "tree wooden blocks." They can also be found on Etsy since they are a hand-crafted item.

These tree wooden blocks pair well with forest animal figures and/or fairy dolls. These wooden blocks, made from real pieces of wood, bark still intact, help children with nature play and imaginative play. They get use of their fine motor skills while playing with these blocks, too. Playtime and nature are always a good match for learning!

60 Princess Accessory Play

Supplies Needed

- ☐ Crowns
- ☐ tiaras
- ☐ play jewelry
- ☐ tutus
- ☐ long gloves
- ☐ boas
- ☐ princess shoes
- ☐ anything princess-like

We have always had a princess bin in our playroom. Whenever we have playdates, it is always used. Brielle and her little friends naturally gravitate toward the bin filled with boas, tutus, crowns, wands, and jewelry. Before they begin playing anything, they want to first dress up and become princesses. Once they are fully accessorized, they are ready to play.

This kind of imaginative play helps spark their creative thought processes. It also makes good use of their fine motor skills, especially if they must fasten any clasps for the jewelry or put on long gloves and work each finger into the correct hole.

Dressing up helps children engage in role play and can transport their imaginations to a different era. They get to have fun, and they are engaging a variety of developmental skills in the process. Dressing up is more than just fun. There is learning going on, too.

We have princess dresses hanging in our playroom closet. Sometimes they get those out at the same time, but not always. The one thing that is always constant is that they all head for the princess accessory bin before they can play with anything else in the playroom. Their work, or playtime, cannot commence until they are fully accessorized.

In the photo shown are some items I recently picked up at the Dollar Tree to replenish our basket of princess accessories. Crowns and wands tend to break or lose gemstones over time. The Dollar Tree or similar retail discount stores are a great place to find new items for replenishment.

61 Sequencing Puzzle Play

Supplies Needed

☐ Sequencing puzzles

There are many sequencing puzzles and activity kits that can be found from educational companies such as Lakeshore Learning. You can also find them on Amazon. These are a great classroom tool and are also a fun learning toy for any home, since they are not an expensive activity. Sequencing puzzles help children learn about numbering and order. This fine motor skill activity is a great introduction to number identification and early counting skills.

Our family picked up some sequencing number puzzles at Target in the Dollar section when they were selling school supplies one fall. My kids are still playing with them two years later. Some puzzles never get old.

62 Grocery Store Pretend Play

Supplies Needed

☐ Price stickers from the Dollar Tree or other discount store

☐ Monopoly money

☐ food items (play or real)

☐ shopping cart shopping bag

☐ toy register or shoe box container and a calculator

Grocery store pretend play needs just a little bit of help from an adult to set up. When we play this at our house, we use play money from our Monopoly game. We put it back after our play time, but it's one less thing to buy that we already own. The small circle stickers I picked up are made for garage sales but work well for our pretend store playtime. These are essentially the only item you will likely need to purchase to make this activity complete. The other items can be found around your home. If you don't have play food items, then you can use real food items from your cabinets or pantry. Put the stickers on each item with a price. If you have a play cash register, it can help this activity become more authentic, but if not, just use a shoe box or Tupperware container. Set the priced items around the room on display for them to shop.

To teach children how to play, have them shop "the store" and then come to your checkout. You can add up all the items. Tell them their total. You should have given your children some play money in advance, which they can take to your store in an old wallet or one of your old purses. This helps to make them feel like mom or dad out shopping.

You can use a calculator to total their items, and then they can give you the play cash. This activity is a great imaginative play activity that also involves role play. Children can take turns being the cashier and shoppers. By having an adult participate with the play activity to show them how the store works, it gets the ball rolling for children to do it on their own. This activity also helps children develop math and counting skills as they use their play money to pay for their food items.

63 Lite-Brite

☐ A Lite-Brite set

Lite-Brite has been around for years. It is another toy that has been all but forgotten. However, it is making a comeback because of its value in developmental learning, and the fun that kids find in creating with this toy. The Lite-Brite involves using round plastic pegs and inserting them into the Lite-Brite screen to make a design of your choosing. When you are complete with your design, you turn off the lights in the room and watch your design illuminate! This activity helps kids develop creative skills. Since these pieces are small and require precise placement into the holes, it is also good practice of fine motor skills, including finger and thumb grasping.

This activity may not be found in all stores, but it can be found online from a variety of makers. If you type in Lite-Brite online, a wide variety of these products will come up.

This activity can be used to write letters, numbers, and words using the pegs, which also helps your child develop letter and number skills. Some occupational therapists use this toy in their practice and recommend it for families to use because it is so beneficial to early childhood development, especially fine motor skill improvement. Because of the way that the pegs must be grasped to insert into the Lite-Brite, it mimics the grasp needed for holding pencils and other writing utensils. Thus, playing with this activity can help develop the tripod grasp that will be so important in their early elementary years. Kids are motivated to play with this activity, because they want to create something that will light up and look magical!

64 Bear Pattern Play

Supplies Needed

☐ Plastic bears and counting/pattern cards

This is a developmental manipulative tool that I learned about at our preschool. These little bears are a popular tool for classroom learning. You can find them in large batches for purchase on Amazon and through other online retailers. You can also purchase them with pattern cards from Amazon. If you want to buy just the bears and print your own pattern cards you can do that, too. Just go to Pinterest and use the term "bear pattern cards" and you will find free printables from a variety of blogs and websites.

This preschool manipulative helps children learn about counting, addition, and patterns. It helps with the development of early math skills. Children are also using their motor skills to play with these bears. It is a simple activity, but one that preschool children truly seem to enjoy and delight in doing! Sometimes the pattern cards will only show the repeating pattern once or twice, and then the child must keep the pattern going on their own. I watched many of the children call out to show off their work to their teacher as they accomplished the patterns on their own. They gained confidence because of their ability to master the pattern cards. **It is wonderful for preschool children to feel a sense of accomplishment and delight in the joy in learning.** It is a feeling that we want children to experience when they are young. When they discover the joy of learning, it will help them become more passionate learners, as they want to replicate this sense of accomplishment in future learning.

65 Costume Play

Supplies Needed

☐ A variety of costumes

Costume play is wonderful for child development. Children use their imagination and creative skills when they get into costume. **Costume play unlocks a child's imagination and opens a world of possibilities just by putting on costumes**. They can become a princess who is locked in a dungeon and is searching for a way out, or they can become a NASA astronaut headed to Mars, or they can become Snow White, and the dolls in front of them are the Seven Dwarfs. The possibilities are almost endless when costumes are brought into playtime, and imaginative play is crucial to their development as creative thinkers.

Because children must push beyond the words that they would typically use to become a pretend character, costume play also helps build their vocabulary. You may hear them use phrases or words that they have heard in books or fairy tales. They broaden their use of vocabulary as they become a different character.

Costume play is also good for social and emotional development. Children will interact with one another in costume playtime. They need social interactions, and costumes can help take their guard down if they are shy or apprehensive about playing with other children. Costumes allow them to pretend that they are someone else, which can unlock a social confidence inside themselves that they didn't know was even there.

Costumes do not need to be an expensive investment. We have a closet filled with dozens of play costumes for both girls and boys. My kids love to dress up. I didn't want to spend a fortune on costumes though. Instead I went on the hunt for secondhand costumes. I found several at a local children's consignment store. I have also purchased costumes from consignment sales for children's items that are held at local convention centers and churches. Be on the lookout for children's consignment sales like Rhea Lana's and Just Between Friends. These companies and others like them are franchises with weekend sales around the country. Even out of season, they will have racks of costumes but are often displayed on Halloween racks. One person's Halloween costume can become part of your child's play costume collection. We also look for used dance costumes. Typically, these are purchased for a small fortune by the original owner and worn once. You can then find them at consignment sales. I have purchased most of ours for prices between $8 and $12, which is remarkable considering many of these costumes were originally purchased for upwards of $100. My daughter is in dance, so we save her dance costumes each year and add them to our collection of dress up clothes in our costume closet.

Another place to look for used costumes is on buy, sell, trade groups on Facebook. I have found some good costumes from friends on these pages, especially after Halloween. I buy them and put them into our costume closet. We have not needed to purchase Halloween costumes for several years, because I tell my kids they can pick their costume from the costume closet in our playroom since there are many there for them to choose from.

Used costumes can always be washed. If you are purchasing them for home use or classroom use, they will look used within a week of play anyway. They will get wear and tear, so if they are purchased gently used, they will fit right in with your existing costumes. Throw them in the washing machine and sew anything that needs to be repaired. The kids will love the costumes whether they are new or gently used.

66 Time Period Imaginative Play

☐ Costumes that help kids imagine themselves in another time period or era

This type of imaginative play is also fantasy play where children get to pretend and allow their imagination to run wild. They pretend that they are from another era when they don the suits of armor and play out a scene in which they are protecting a king and his queen from dragons. This imaginative role play helps to stimulate their creative thought processes. You can always make costumes from cardboard and other household items. Pinterest offers many ideas for homemade costumes. The sky is the limit! Whatever helps children get into this kind of role play activity and boosts their imagination is great for brain development.

If you decide to make your own costumes from Pinterest let your child get in on the fun with their own ideas. Sometimes creating the costumes and accessories is more fun for some children than the actual playtime.

If you are more of an Amazon Prime parent than a Pinterest parent, then you can find these suits of armor by searching "knights' suit play costume" on Amazon and you will find plenty of options. When you type in these key words you may also get astronaut suits, as I did. Those are another great imaginative play costume that will open up the world of astronomy, rocketry, and space to your children.

67 Career Costume Role Play

Supplies Needed

☐ A set of career costumes

This is the kind of activity where I become more of an Amazon Prime mom rather than a Pinterest mom. However, if you would rather create career costumes you can certainly go to Pinterest and find ideas on how to create your own. Personally, I find that the easy way for this one is just a click away on Amazon. Just use the search phrase "career costumes" and you will find sets of career costumes available for purchase.

Princess and superhero costumes are very popular, but career costumes can be too if they are available to your children in your home or classroom. Kids get the opportunity to role play when they put on these costumes. They can become a vet, doctor, police officer, chef, a cowboy, or whatever the simple costume may represent. It is remarkable how such a simple thing as a costume vest or top can transport a child and their imagination to another realm.

Role play is an important part of early childhood development as it helps children build confidence and imaginative skills. They can act out real life roles when donning simple costumes. They can also put on performances using these costumes, which is also beneficial to their development.

The social interactions that occur during role play are very important to their development. When they role play, children learn how to interact with their peers, handle conflict, and how to engage in productive play. It can also help them develop empathy as they take on roles as doctors or firemen and act out saving others in distress. **Role play is crucial to childhood development because this type of play is a child's way of practicing for real life.**

68 Button Lacing

Supplies Needed

☐ Extra-large buttons and string for lacing

You can find these extra-large buttons and the strings for purchase as kits on Amazon. Just use the search phrase "button lacing" and you will find lots of options. This is another preschool manipulative that engages children and gets them using fine motor skills on their own. They love to sort the buttons by color, create patterns by color and shape, and then lace them together using the string. This is a reusable toy that lasts for years. It is an inexpensive manipulative as well.

Kids will strengthen their hand and finger muscles while playing with this activity. It is also good practice for their fine motor pincer grasp. This activity will help them develop their hand muscles and grasping skills, which will help them properly hold pencils and learn writing skills in the future.

This activity also requires concentration as they must focus on putting the string though the small holes to lace the buttons together. It is a great manipulative that fits in a small container for storage, it is expensive, and has many benefits for a child's development. This is a good one for both preschool and home use.

Don't give away the buttons when they no longer play with them. Save them for their 100 days of school projects. If they must decorate a shirt with 100 items, these buttons will come in handy someday. You don't need to sew them either. Use fabric glue that also bonds to plastic and you are set!

69 Bounce House Fun!

❑ A bounce house

I debated whether to include this one, but then I remembered how many of my friends purchased a bounce house after they saw how much fun their kids had playing in ours. Our bounce house was purchased for my daughter's first birthday. We have been using it ever since, and she is now seven! We purchased ours from Amazon. I had checked prices for renting a bounce house for her birthday party and realized that for the cost of renting twice we could own our own bounce house; albeit a smaller house than the ones that you rent, nevertheless the kids have had many a joyful day bouncing till they dropped. This was a good buy for our family, and we have used it dozens of times when friends have come over for play dates. We also set it up in our foyer of our home for playtime on cold winter days when they had more energy than I knew how to handle. It has literally been used at least 100 times, and we have never had any problems with it either.

Of course, there is a risk of injury with bounce houses so be aware of the risks and dangers associated with bounce house play. Always supervise children while they play in a bounce house. In addition, always stake down an outdoors bounce house because there are horror stories of them blowing away with children inside. Use bounce houses with caution and care if you do decide to buy one. We never had any injuries with ours, but I always set rules regarding the number of children allowed to play at one time, and we implemented a no touching policy while inside the bounce house. Read all the warnings and cautions that come with your bounce house, as there are genuine risks involved with bounce houses and kids.

We purchased ours despite the risks, but always had an adult supervising and explained the rules to the kids before they played. Bounce houses are great for gross motor skill development such as balancing and jumping. It is also a fun way for children to engage their vestibular system, which is responsible for much of their physical, emotional, and learning development. Jumping, spinning, and swinging are the most common physical activities that stimulate the vestibular system. Bounce houses obviously make for lots of jumping; therefore, a great deal of vestibular stimulation happens with this kind of activity.

70  Post Office

- ☐ Cardboard box
- ☐ blue wrapping paper
- ☐ envelopes
- ☐ small packages
- ☐ blank paper for writing letters
- ☐ bins for sorting mail
- ☐ a small scale if you have one

Our preschool had a mail station as one of their activity centers this past school year. The kids loved it so much we decided to create one for our home, too. This activity is great for role play, as children imagine what it would be like to work at a post office and the duties it would entail. Our preschool went on a tour of our local post office and got to see firsthand how everything works behind the scenes. Having firsthand knowledge of the post office and seeing it for themselves made this play activity come to life for my children even more.

To create a post office, you need sorting baskets and you can label them "In Town", "Out of Town", and "Packages." This is much like the sorting they do at the post office counters when they receive items from customers. We also own a table scale, so my kids use that to weigh packages that they stuffed full of toys that they imagined they were shipping to their cousins. It gets their cognitive skills working, along with some thoughtfulness tied into the play, as they try to imagine which cousins would like which of their toys.

The mailbox is simple to create. First, we bought solid blue wrapping paper. Next, we cut an opening for the mail and left the bottom of the box open so that they could lift the box to retrieve the letters. We wrapped the box, leaving the opening for the mail and then wrote "Mail" on a piece of paper and glued it to the front of the box.

This role play fun also helps children with their fine motor skill development as they sort through the mail. They can also be given stickers to use as stamps. Sticker play also helps with fine motor skill development.

This is also a good opportunity for children to practice their writing skills, as they write letters to send to loved ones. If they can't write words yet, they can practice their name and draw a picture to mail. This activity is helpful for letter writing practice and gets their creative skills working at the same time.

71 Count and Add Matching

☐ The Learning Journey Match It-Numbers

☐ Fun-to Know Puzzles Numbers 1-20

☐ Melissa & Doug Self-Correcting Number Puzzles or other number-matching activity kits of this kind

I listed several options for this preschool-age activity in the necessary supplies listed above. These are three different types found on Amazon, and you can find a variety of others online as well. I provided the specific names of three of these activities to make it easier for you to find them online so you can search by their exact name, but they are all similar and teach children numbers and counting in the same manner.

Count and Add Matching has been a popular manipulative at our preschool. The kids would get into groups of three or four and work on these puzzles together. The activity involves matching with numbers. One piece of the puzzle has a number. They need to look for the matching puzzle piece that has that specific number of objects. For example, the number four matches with the puzzle piece that has four burgers.

This activity is a fine motor skill activity that helps children learn number identification and develops their counting skills. It is a helpful tool for teaching early math skills. It is also a good team activity, as I watched it being used by children in small groups at our preschool. I was impressed how they worked cooperatively and helped one another find the pieces that they were looking for to complete their puzzle or their friend's puzzle.

72 Car Racetrack

☐ Matchbox cars and a car rug

My boys love to play with cars. At home we have hundreds of Matchbox cars that they have collected over the years. It seems that every birthday and holiday they get more of them as gifts. We have used the Matchbox racetrack pieces, but they always require my involvement and lots of time. Racetracks are a great way to play with cars and I recommend them. However, using an area rug as a racetrack is a pure genius idea that is an easy way to get them imagining and racing their cars, but without having to pull out the plastic tracks that require assembly and thus lots of your time.

Playing with cars is a great way to get children using their hands and developing both their fine motor and gross motor skills. Children love to get cars rolling, testing them to see which cars are faster than others, and how fast they will go on different surfaces, such as tables, carpeting, etc. **The experimenting and learning that goes on with children and their car play is vaster than we realize as parents.** Playing with cars helps with cognitive and physical development; it is more than just play for entertainment purposes.

Letting children explore with their cars on different surfaces and in different ways, such as pushing around toys with the cars or knocking down blocks, helps children in their cognitive development. They are learning how things work with this type of play. Encourage their exploration by providing them a variety of areas and spaces for them to explore with their cars. The rug is a good and safe place to get started for little kids, but they will want to try out their cars in other places before long.

73 Pediatrician or Vet Imaginative Play

☐ Play doctor's kit and dolls or stuffed animals

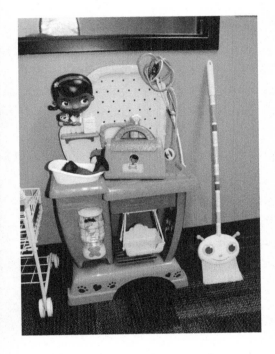

The photo shown was an activity center at our preschool. The Doc McStuffins exam table was a nice touch to make it more fun, but the table is not necessary for kids to play this kind of activity. All your child will need for this activity is a play doctor's kit and some dolls or stuffed animals for them to use as patients. A stethoscope, blood pressure cuff, reflex hammer, and ear scope are the most common items sold in play doctor kits. There are some that come with over 20 items in their kits that you can find on Amazon or in toy stores, as play doctor kits have been popular for decades.

This activity helps children with their imaginative and role-play development. They can pretend that they are a doctor or nurse and are doing a general exam on a baby or an animal. They get to use tools like they have seen their doctor use on them. This activity also helps deal with any anxiousness that they may feel from going to the doctor since they become more familiar with the tools and actions that take place in a doctor's office.

You can play with your child and pretend that you are the patient. You will be surprised with the creative things your child will think up with this kind of play activity.

This activity helps with their fine motor skills as they use the play medical tools. It is also a good activity to help them develop empathy and practice caring for others. **Even if it is imaginative play, it is practice for real life.**

74 Hairdresser

☐ Dolls with hair or a Barbie hair styling head

Barbie hair styling heads were around when I was a kid and are still great toys and wonderful tools for getting kids using their fine motor skills. It is also an activity that can be used to teach them about hygiene and hair care. If you don't have a Barbie hair styling head, you can have your child use a Barbie doll or other doll with hair. You can provide them with some hairbrushes, barrettes, combs, hair ties, curlers, etc. The key is to provide a variety of tools and accessories so they can practice playing with their doll head and develop fine motor skills as they play with various small items that require finger manipulation to use them. Different barrettes may require opening and closing in different ways as their closures vary. This variety helps them practice and use their little hands to manipulate numerous items in different ways.

They can practice doing the doll's hair. You can also use this as a teaching opportunity. They may not know how to create a ponytail, but you can show them how it is done. This is a great way to teach them how to braid, if they are ready for that level of skill. Again, it is an opportunity for you to teach, and then allow them to play on their own and try these skills out for themselves.

This activity may look like it is more fun than learning, but there is developmental learning taking place. Their fine motor skills are being used as they put barrettes in the doll's hair and manipulate twist ties around bunches of hair. It is a skill building play time. They also are using their creativity to make different styles on the doll, which helps with cognitive development.

If you are brave enough, you can have your child practice on your hair as well. It is a good bonding experience and confidence-building activity. They will love playing with your hair more than a doll's hair but be prepared because it likely won't be as gentle as your own hairdresser!

75 Foam Sand

Supplies Needed

☐ 8 cups of play sand
☐ one 10-ounce can of foaming shaving cream

We purchased play sand at Walmart, and it was very inexpensive. The shaving cream we had on hand, but you can purchase a can at the Dollar Tree or wherever you typically shop. It can be cheap shaving cream, but it needs to be the cream and not a gel.

This activity is a sensory play experience. Let the kids mix up the ingredients using their hands. We used a large Rubbermaid bin, like the size you place under a bed for storage. This type of bin is shallow enough to allow their arms inside for playing with the sand and yet also large enough to give them space to manipulate and play with the sand.

This is a good activity and material to use for writing numbers and letters. Once the mixture is completely combined, they can write with their fingers in the sand. It is a great opportunity to have them practice their name or specific letters of the alphabet in the foam sand.

Playing in this sand mixture and using it as an opportunity to practice writing letters, shapes, numbers, or words is wonderful for fine motor skill development. This sensory exploration activity is sure to get some smiles and giggles because it is like handling chocolate mousse that has grit. It is a neat experience that you will want to try for yourself as well. It may look like mousse, but don't let the kids eat it!

The shaving cream will dissolve after a few days. You can leave it out in the sun to let it dry out, and it can then be used for regular sand play. We played with this activity inside on the first day. Thereafter we took it outside for playtime, as it is a messier activity.

76 Dauber Art

Supplies Needed

☐ Daubers (these are dot markers in a variety of colors) and dot marker printables

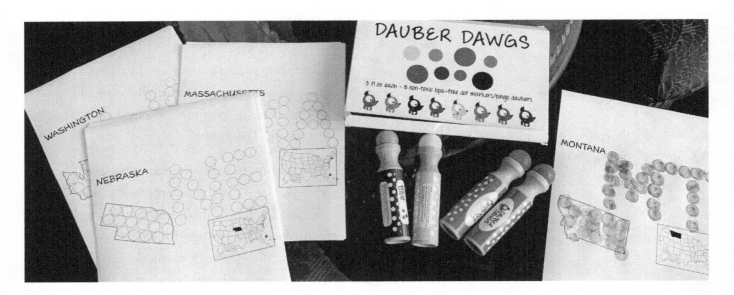

Daubers are also known as dot markers, bingo daubers, and crazy dot markers. They come in regular size and a miniature size as well. The regular size is what you would see people using as they play competitive Bingo. When searching for this product on Amazon you can use the term "daubers" and you will find lots of options. I personally prefer washable daubers. That way if kids make a mess it is easier to clean and more likely to wash out of clothing.

The dauber set we purchased came with a link for free printable sheets to download. This allowed me to print multiple copies of each page, so my kids didn't have to argue over who got to do which sheet. You can search "dot marker printables free" on Pinterest and you will find plenty of sheets to print for your children, many of which have an educational theme. On Pinterest, I was able to find printable dot marker sheets with shapes, numbers, Disney characters, letters, bugs, flowers, dinosaurs, and more. There are also some sheets that are activities. For example, one was an ice cream cone counting activity. It had cones with a number on the bottom of the cone and that number reflected the number of dots on the ice cream that were to be filled in. Two dots for the ice cream cone labeled with number two, three dots for the ice cream cone labeled with a three, etc. These activities help with learning, and they are also helpful for motor skill development. Dexterity is improved as they learn to use the markers and place dots within each circle. This requires some practice and hand-and-eye coordination. It is also an opportunity to make creative choices with colors and how they use the daubers.

The great thing about daubers is that they seem to last forever. We have had ours for about three years now and not one has dried up! They have gotten plenty of use too! I also like the fact that the clean-up is easy for this project, yet the kids still get to be expressive and creative.

77 Phone Number Play

☐ Paper plates
☐ a marker

☐ painters' tape (or other tape that is safe for wall use)

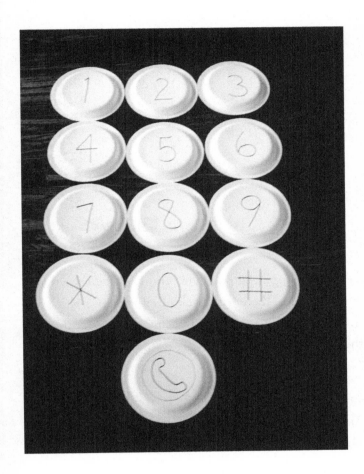

This activity can help teach children number recognition. It can also be used to teach children about reacting to an emergency and how to dial 911. Helping them memorize their parent's phone number with this visual and interactive activity is also great for kids.

To create this activity, you simply write the numbers and symbols, as shown, on the backside of paper plates. I used the dial screen from my Smart phone as our example since this is what my kids are used to seeing. Once you have this done you can tape them to a wall using tape that won't damage the wall, such as blue painters' tape.

You can have the kids practice tapping the numbers as you tell them the phone numbers. They can take turns. This helps them with number recognition and is also good practice for learning to dial numbers. Their gross motor skills are also used for this activity, as they reach and jump to press the numbers on the wall.

78 Story Telling: Create Your Own Book

Supplies Needed

☐ Blank books and markers or other writing utensils

These blank books can typically be found in stores when school supplies go on sale. The package shown was purchased at Target. It contains eight books that have 16 pages each. The entire pack of eight books was $3. I purchased five of these packs, and this is the last one left unopened. The rest have all been used up over the past nine months. This activity is a great way for kids to use their storytelling skills to write a story or draw it out in pictures. All three of my kids love making these books.

You can always make your own booklets by folding papers together and stapling it in the center. It doesn't need to be complicated or fancy, and yet something so simple can get your kids thinking, developing stories, drawing, and creating. This kind of imaginative work is beneficial to their cognitive development, fine motor development, and writing skills.

Reading books to children is crucial to their development. Creating stories and the ability to re-tell stories that they have heard is also of great benefit. If they can't think of their own stories, have them re-tell stories that they know by heart. You can also give them themes. A Christmas theme or Santa Claus stories seem to get my children thinking creatively and inventing their own stories.

Another creative writing or storytelling practice is to have them tell stories from their personal life experiences. Perhaps they can write about or draw their first trip to Disney World or what they did on their summer vacation. Whatever can get them thinking about process, story flow, and making sense of their thoughts for others to understand is helpful to their cognitive development. They also get to utilize problem-solving skills as they create a plot because even a simple plot requires resolution to finish the story.

Here are some tips for creating a story that you can use to help your child create their own story:

1. Think of an idea or theme. If they have difficulty coming up with something, talk about their own experiences, such as trips they have been on or exciting things that have happened to them.

2. Determine the main characters and the setting. When and where is this story taking place? Help them describe their character by asking some questions. How old is your character? What is their name? What do they look like? Is there something that makes them unique or special?

3. Decide how the story will begin. Where does the story start? What is the main character doing as the story begins?

4. Define the conflict. Every good story has a conflict or a situation to overcome. It could be something as simple as Sally lost her favorite teddy bear.

5. Write about the character's reaction, what was felt in this moment of conflict. How did the character react in the situation? What emotions did he or she feel? How did their reaction affect the situation, good or bad?

6. Describe the turning point. This is where things change, and the resolution is on the horizon.

7. The resolution. Describe how the problem is resolved. This is when they can describe how the character felt and acted once the problem was solved.

If your child can't write yet, they can still create the illustrations. You can help them write the story. Use their words, and write the story down in their book for them. Make it a fun activity that gets them thinking creatively or reminiscing about their life experiences that they can share in the book.

When you help children develop their own writing skills, they tend to become more interested in reading books and stories. **Creating a passion in your child for reading and writing starts with igniting a love for storytelling at a young age.** Help your child by not only reading books often to them, but also help them write and create their own stories. They have the imagination; you just need to help guide them by asking some open-ended questions to get the ball rolling.

79 DIY Ball Toss

Supplies Needed

☐ Buckets and Ping-Pong balls

This is a simple game, yet my kids are obsessed. They will literally argue over who gets to go next. This game is very easy to learn. Even very young kids can participate. Simply line up the buckets, the one closest to the kids will have the lowest point value. I used values 1-4, but you can use tens or even hundreds. Whatever you want to label the buckets is up to you. The important factor is that the bucket with the highest value is furthest from where the children will be tossing the balls. I sometimes lay down a stick on the ground, so that they know they must stand behind that makeshift line. Kids that are significantly younger than the others can move closer to the buckets.

Ping-Pong balls are perfect for this activity. You can also put some sand in the bottom of the buckets, so the balls don't bounce out as often. It depends on the bucket whether you will have a big or little bounce effect. Some bounce is fine, but if every ball bounces out you probably need some sand in the buckets, or even something soft like socks, so that the balls don't bounce out.

This is an activity we like to do while camping. The kids keep track of their points. Each turn they get to throw three Ping-Pong balls. They add up the score from those three tosses. For example, if they made it into the buckets with two out of the three balls with one landing in bucket three and the other landing in bucket one, then they earned four points that round. You can decide how many rounds to go, or you can say that the first person to get to twenty wins. That is usually how we play.

This activity helps with hand-eye coordination, focus, depth perception, and is fun for all ages. We have played various versions of this game with our kids while camping and with other families too. Both kids and adults can play, making it a great social activity. The kids get exercise too, because we always make them run after the balls that bounce away. This is fun for all ages and can help children developmentally through the process of playing.

80 Letter Water Scoop

☐ Plastic magnetic letters   ☐ a bin to hold water   ☐ a scoop

This activity uses plastic magnetic letters. These are the kind that many of us had on our refrigerator as kids, or maybe you have them on your refrigerator now. You fill a bin with water, in our case we used a dishpan from the Dollar Tree. I then added the magnetic letters to the water and gave my child a scoop. I asked him to look for the letters that spell out his name. He was able to scoop out all the letters to spell Charlie, but it took some time and concentration. He was successful in the end though! This activity helps children with letter recognition, hand-eye coordination, focus, and concentration. This fine motor activity also helps with early spelling skills. You can use two bins of water and it can be used as a sorting activity, too. They can sort by color, or they can sort vowels from consonants. Instead of a spoon for scooping you can also have the child use tongs. Plastic tongs will help them with hand muscle strength development.

81 Magnet Play

Supplies Needed   ☐ Magnets with numbers and/or letters and a magnet board

Magnet play and learning go hand in hand. Kids like to play with magnets so providing them with magnets that have numbers and letters makes way for learning to happen. When we play with this magnet board at our home, I let the kids play freely for some time. Then I will ask if they can find the letters for their name and spell it out. An activity like this that involves hunting and finding is good for helping improve their searching skills. It is especially useful if they are the type of child that always seems to be losing their backpack, shoes, bathing suit, or whatever the item may be. They get to practice searching and they also learn number and letter recognition skills in the process. They may need your help, depending on their age, but help as little as possible so they can get a lot out of the learning experience. To struggle and persevere is to gain confidence and learn. **A bit of struggle, especially in this type of controlled learning and play environment is beneficial to the child.**

If the child seems to get frustrated, talk to them about focusing and show them how they can sort through the letters, discarding letters they don't need in one pile and setting aside the ones that they need in another. Such simple lessons can greatly help them learn order, arranging, and sorting skills. This activity also helps with their fine motor skill development and creativity.

We used Disney character magnets for our playtime. Charlie decided that he wanted to spell out the character names after we did his own name. It was fun and educational for him, as he didn't know how to spell any other name than his own. This practice allowed him to spell Pluto and Donald with a little help from me on sounding out the names. It was up to him to find each letter and put them in order.

This magnet board is one I purchased several years back on Amazon. It folds flat for easy storage, and it also doubles as a dry erase board. It is double sided, so two children can play at the same time. It can also be folded into the shape of an easel for drawing artwork using dry erase markers. To find this on Amazon simply search for "Folding Kid's Magnet Board." A few years back we had an easel in our playroom that was chalkboard/magnetic. However, it took up a great deal of space and was often in the way, so the folding magnet board has been much more useful and costs a lot less than an easel.

82 Air Dry Clay

☐ Air Dry Clay

Air dry clay is a great way for children to use their fine motor skills and enhance creativity at the same time. The molding and manipulation of the clay is wonderful for developing their hand and finger strength. This brand of Crayola Air-Dry Clay works great for children. Like the name suggests, it is clay that air dries! No kiln or heat is needed.

As you get started, ensure that the surface where the kids are going to work is completely clean. There is nothing worse than having a three-year-old melt down because a small piece of cereal or debris is stuck in their clay project and it can't be fixed. Avoid a meltdown by making sure the working surface is washed and clean. Also have the children wash their hands before they begin to work with the clay.

You can provide some directions on what they are to create. Small figures and miniature bowls are easier items for them to create. **When children learn how to create with their own hands, they develop a sense of accomplishment, which boosts their self-confidence**. You can jump on Pinterest and find more creative ideas for your kids. Make sure that the projects are appropriate for their age. You want them to feel confident in their skills and that they can execute a project. Small children need simpler ideas and projects. The goal is to have fun, so allow them to utilize their fine motor skills, and strengthen their hand and finger muscles while working with the clay. Just be sure to use their creativity to make something special.

As the clay begins to dry you may see some cracks develop from the drying process. Have a small bowl of water nearby as the children work. That way you or the children can dip your fingers in the water and then smooth out the clay where you see any cracks.

Allow 72 hours for the items to fully dry. They will be breakable, so tell the children they must be gentle and handle with care. The items can be painted after that 72-hour dry time. The nice thing about Crayola Air-Dry Clay is that it comes in white. It dries to a light grey, but it is easy to paint over. This becomes a two-part activity, because they first create something with the clay, and then a few days later they can paint their object.

83 Paper Airplanes

☐ Paper

Making and playing with paper airplanes helps children develop their fine motor skills and hand-eye coordination. They get to practice their throwing and launching skills. They also get some exercise as they run after their airplanes after each throw.

Use lightweight paper to make the airplanes more successful in flying. There are a variety of ways to fold paper to make an airplane; the photo is one example. If you can't seem to make one yourself (and you must be able to do it yourself in order to teach the children), then pull up some YouTube videos. You will find instructions on basic paper airplanes and more elaborate designs. Start simple to get the ball rolling with this activity. Teach the kids how to fold, and then let them experiment with flying their airplanes. Outdoors is typically a good idea unless you have a long straight hallway to utilize.

You can also have the kids color and design their airplanes. This makes it even more fun. They create ownership of their plane as they use their artistic and creative skills to make it just the way they want it to appear.

If the kids get into the activity, watch some additional YouTube videos to learn some more ways to fold and design paper airplanes. You can then go about making these planes, or have the kids help. Once you have several designs completed, you can test them out with the kids to see which ones fly the best. Some may go further, and some may go higher, it's all about experimenting with the planes and trying to get the best throwing action for the greatest results.

84 Gear Play

❑ A set of toy gears

We first discovered this activity in the waiting room at our vet's office. My kids loved it, and it was apparent how much they were learning from it, so I purchased a set for our home. The set we bought was the Kaleido Gears, which is appropriate for children ages 3-7.

This kit will teach children how to assemble and construct gears that work together. When they are connected together correctly the gears will spin at the same time. They will delight in their success when they create a working set of gears! The pieces are easy enough for young hands to manage.

When children play with toy gears, they are using their fine motor skills, engineering skills, imagination, hand-eye coordination, and hand dexterity. It is an activity chock full of developmental benefits! They are also learning the basic mechanics of how gears function.

There are a variety of gear toys that are on the market. My kids have enjoyed playing with our Kaleido Gears (made by Quercetti) for two years.

85 Foam Sticker Art

Supplies Needed

☐ Foam stickers and paper

Foam sticker art projects have been my go-to playdate crafting activity since my children were toddlers. This is something that children can do before they are even able to color with crayons. The littlest children may need help removing the plastic backing from the stickers, but you can hand the foam sticker back to the child, and they can place it where they want on the paper. Except for the sticker backings, foam sticker art involves very little mess. I typically set a basket on the center of the art table for garbage.

Foam sticker art is a great fine motor skill that gets children's fingers working, and with focus. As I noted, removing sticker backings is challenging for most small children, but give them the opportunity to try to do it themselves. If they ask for help, then help them. Otherwise, give them the chance to challenge their motor skills.

The Dollar Tree is a great place to find bags of foam stickers for $1. They typically have letters, numbers, and seasonal collections. This is also a great activity to have on hand for rainy days. The foam stickers are more special that coloring books, at least for my children. They love creating cards and works of art for family and friends using foam stickers on colored construction paper.

If children are utilizing number and letter stickers, they are also getting to practice identification of numbers and letters, and perhaps even spelling out their own name. It is a fun way to work with letters and an opportunity to teach them while they are creating their work of art.

For the older kids, I will bring out glue and larger foam cutouts that don't have the sticker backing. This is good practice for other skills such as working with glue, including evenly distributing it, and using pressure to adhere the foam pieces together. It is also a good time for them to experiment. In the photo for this activity, you can see my son Alex was trying to see how many layers of foam he could get to stick together. **Children are always trying out new ideas and processes in their play and art activities, which is the method by which they learn how things work.** Play is learning, so allow them the space and opportunity to do these projects and to experiment if they so desire.

86 Move it Sticks

Supplies Needed ☐ Extra Large Popsicle Sticks and a Marker

Do you want your kids to burn off some of their energy? This is the perfect activity to get kids moving. When we use move it sticks at home, we pretend that the kids are at school and its P.E. (physical education) time. We use our move sticks with a timer, but you can easily use your phone and set a timer for 30, 45, or 60 seconds. The kids each select a move it stick, and they do that activity for the time period that you chose. You can vary time periods to make it more interesting. My kids like doing everything for points and making activities more of a competition. We awarded one point per activity that they completed for the duration of the time period. If they quit before the timer went off, then they didn't get the point. Ten or fifteen minutes of this activity will get them to burn off a lot of energy and help them do a calmer sit-down activity afterwards. We went inside after doing this for fifteen minutes. Brielle won the contest, as she completed every move it stick for the full duration. Alex came in second place, only quitting once! Charlie, well Charlie was more interested in playing with the dog and only finished about half of his activities, but he still burned off plenty of energy and got lots of exercise.

This activity is helpful for developing gross motor skills. It is also an activity that provides plenty of exercise for kids. This helps to get them moving and prevents childhood obesity, which is a rising problem in America.

How exactly can this activity provide so much exercise you say? These are the activities we wrote on our sticks: bear crawl, star jumps, skaters, high knees, frog jumps, squats, pushup jumps, run in place, pushups, crab walk, jumping jacks, and high jumps!

87 War

Supplies Needed

☐ A deck of cards

While camping with another family, their mom brought out a deck of cards to play war with the kids. We got to talking and she told me that while she was substituting at her child's preschool, they played war in the classroom as a learning activity. What a great idea! My kids love to play war with me, and we play at least several times a week. Now I recognize what a great learning activity it is as well!

When kids play war, they are learning about number identification and number order. They will learn very quickly that a ten is higher than a two and that an eight will beat a seven because it is higher. To be honest, I hadn't realized that was exactly how my kids had learned about number value until that conversation with my friend.

This simple card game requires no complex skills or strategy. It is a great way to get small children learning their numbers through play. They are also using their fine motor skills to handle the cards. When my kids first started to play war their fine motor skills were weak. It was difficult for them to hold on to the slippery cards, and to separate them from each other. But after a few rounds, I saw how their fine motor skills dramatically improved. They were able to separate the cards with their fingers more easily and they even learned how to shuffle on their own!

Playing war is simple. You use and shuffle an entire deck of cards (we include Jokers and they win against any number). For two players you split the deck in half, so each player has an equal number of cards. Each player has their stack of cards face down in front of them. Each player then turns over their first card. Whoever has the highest card wins both cards. The winner sweeps their cards to their side for later use. This continues until one player wins all the cards. When all the cards in the stacks are used up, they shuffle the cards that they won and use them as their new stack.

War occurs when the players have the same card come up. For example, both players flip over playing cards with the number five in the same turn. Players then each put down three more cards, face down, so neither player can see these cards. Next, they flip a fourth card. This card determines the winner of all the cards laid down during the war. That means one player will win all ten cards (five from each player). Double war is also possible, meaning twenty cards are at stake. Triple war has happened to us just once or twice. This means that matching cards were turned over three times in a row and thirty cards were at stake for one winner to take all.

You can play this game with or without face cards. If you just want your children to learn the numbers, you can remove the face cards. You will then be left with a deck of cards that has numbers two through ten. If you have more than four people playing you will want to use two decks of cards.

The goal of the game is to be the player who wins all the cards. Once one player wins all the cards the game is over. **Card playing is fun and helps children learn their numbers while also improving their fine motor skills.** Don't do the work for them. Let them handle their own cards so they learn how to manage them with their own hands. It may take some work and effort on their part, but that is exactly how their fine motor skills can develop.

88 UNO

☐ A set of UNO cards

UNO is a card game. We have two versions of UNO at our home, as shown in the photo. They both are essentially played in the same manner. UNO sells a variety of themed decks. In order to play this game, you will need one set of UNO cards, which is different than a regular deck of cards.

I am not going to explain all the rules because they come with the game if you choose to buy it. You can also find the rules online.

This is a great game for young children to play because it teaches them about numbers, colors, and matching them together. For example, on a blue five the next player can either play a blue card or the number five in any color. If they don't have either in their hand, then they draw a card. This game helps with number and color identification for children. As they learn to play, they find there is some strategy involved. As they get better at the game, they will think about which cards to play that will help them win the game and which cards to play so that someone else doesn't win. It gets their cognitive wheels turning!

This is a highly social activity. I grew up in a household that plays games. I have always told my husband that our family will play games together, too. And we do. Games are a way to come together, engage one another, and have fun at the same time! The goal is social interaction and fun, but the children are also learning in the process.

Children are also using their fine motor skills when playing this game as they hold all their playing cards in their hands. Unlike war, where the cards remain face down until one is played, UNO requires that players hold their cards in their hands so that other players cannot see what is on the cards. That means this game teaches children how to manipulate and properly hold the cards, which improves their fine motor skills.

Playing card games or board games also provides the opportunity to teach children about sportsmanship. They can be taught how to congratulate other children who win and to not act negatively when they personally lose. **It is good practice for life when they lose at a game, because they learn that they cannot be the winner every time**. Being a good sport while losing is not easy for most children. This can be discussed while playing games, and they can practice using good sportsmanship skills during a game.

89 Creature Sand Search

Supplies Needed

☐ Bin for sand play
☐ play sand

☐ a variety of plastic creatures (lizards, bugs, etc.)

This activity involves sensory play, but it is also good for fine motor skill development. Putting everything needed in a bin makes it a reusable play activity. Sandboxes outside tend to be too big for this activity. The best way to store them is in a container that fits under a bed. They are just the right size for children to reach in and play, yet wide and long enough to hold plenty of sand and toys.

Children can also be given sifters to use in this activity and shovels for digging. These tools are good for fine motor development and dexterity skills. You can make it a matching game by taking photos of each item and putting them onto a sheet of paper. Then they search in the sand for the items on the sheet. Once they find the item, they lay it on the sheet on top of the photo of that item. This activity helps them with their matching skills. You can even laminate the sheet, so it is good for many future uses.

You can purchase play sand by the bag at most home improvement stores. We picked up one bag at Walmart, which was more than enough for our bin. I ordered it with our Walmart grocery pickup, which meant I didn't have to go into the store to find it. A Walmart employee loaded it into my trunk when I picked up my grocery order.

Once they find all the creatures, they can then have some free play with the sand, creatures, shovels, and sifters. This allows them to play creatively and use their imagination.

90 Handprint and Footprint Projects

☐ Non-toxic poster paint for making the handprints or footprints on paper (or other items for putting the prints on, such as glass tile and plates, in which case you need paints that work for glass)

What parent doesn't cherish artwork that was created using their child's handprints or footprints? Here are just a few examples of what you can create. Using the paint on their hands or feet to create handprints or footprints on paper is good sensory play for children. It also involves good use of their hand-eye coordination as they try to create prints that look great. After they make their print on the paper and the artwork is complete, allow the children to continue to paint with their hands and finger on other papers. It is a great way to allow them to think creatively and experiment with this sensory play activity.

91 Pom Sorting

Supplies Needed

☐ Fluffy poms in a variety of colors and sizes

☐ a container that has sections for sorting

☐ plastic tongs

It is remarkable to me how such a simple activity kit that is so inexpensive can keep my son Charlie entertained for so long. Not just once or twice either. He asks to play with this kit daily. I won't let him play with it unless he asks, as this one could be dumped out and get lost among toys and other items quite easily. We have a plastic shoebox bin for this activity, and he plays with it for about a half hour at a time and then we put it away. Charlie is the most active of all my children. I sometimes wonder where he gets all the energy! This is one activity that I know he enjoys doing and it makes him calm, quiet, and focused for a half hour or more at one time. This activity is like a miracle in a shoebox bin!

I purchased the poms at both the Dollar Tree and Walmart. The tongs came from the Dollar Tree (in their party section). The plastic sorting container was also a Dollar Tree purchase. This activity cost less than $5 total and it has been worth every penny! There are similar manipulatives you can get from preschool supply companies, but this one is cheap and easy to make yourself.

Children can sort by color, size, or both. Sometimes Charlie plays with it and tries to see how many he can collect in the tongs at one time. This activity helps with the development of fine motor skills, hand-eye coordination, focus, patience, counting, and sorting skills.

92 Restaurant

☐ Play dishware   ☐ chairs   ☐ notepad with pencil for the waitress
☐ play food items   ☐ apron
☐ table

This is a fun role play activity that gets kids thinking about what it would be like to work in a restaurant as a cook, waitress, or busboy. The kids can take turns playing different roles, each getting to be the demanding customer at least once. This activity helps them to play imaginatively while also re-creating a restaurant experience as authentic as possible. You can allow them to use food if you are present and want to be more involved in their play activity. My kids liked the play food items, but my daughter Brielle is very literal on everything. She brought the entire container of play food items out for her customer, Alex, to make his selections. He then had to remember them so she could fetch her notepad and pencil to write the order down. His requests had to only be choices for the play items we had on hand. Charlie was the cook and got to pretend to prepare the food items in our play kitchen.

This is a good play activity that encourages social interaction and teamwork. The restaurant employees (cook, cashier, busboy, cooks, waitresses) must all work together to serve the customer. It is fun and a good learning experience for kids. Depending on their role, they will likely get to use their fine motor and planning skills while executing this play activity.

93 Mosaic Sticker Artwork

☐ Mosaic sticker art kit

This is a wonderful fine-motor activity that helps children develop dexterity of their fingers. Picking up the tiny stickers and placing them on the artwork in the right spot requires focus and attention to detail.

You can find mosaic sticker artwork kits at craft stores, Amazon, and the Dollar Tree, to name just a few options. This type of artwork will keep children busy and focused for longer than you think. There are mosaic sticker art kits in a variety of characters and themes. We found a tiara mosaic sticker art kit, which we purchased for Brielle's birthday party a few years ago. Each guest got to decorate their own tiara using the mosaic stickers.

There are varying degrees of difficulty for these art sets, so be sure to select the mosaic sticker artwork kit that is best for your child's age and skill level. This activity is not good for very small children who put things in their mouth. There are simply too many small pieces, which are a hazard if swallowed.

To get the kids started you may need to help them see which stickers go where. They are often numbered on the artwork, and certain stickers are to be used on specific numbers. Once they get going, they can do it on their own. They will gain self-confidence when they complete one of these projects, too!

94 Marble Run

☐ A marble run kit and marbles

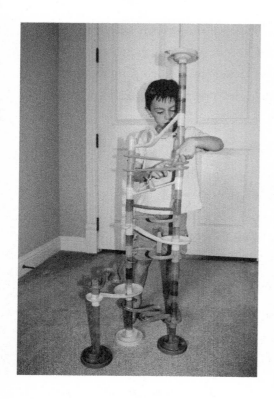

A marble run is a fantastic toy for helping children develop their engineering skills. This toy requires focus, concentration, and some trial-and-error to successfully create a working marble run. This activity can help them gain confidence and self-esteem when they are successful in making the apparatus work.

When children work together to create a marble run, it becomes a great activity for learning teamwork. As they work cooperatively, they are learning from another and working as a team to maximize their success.

This activity also helps with memory and recall development. Each time they play with this toy they will get better at assembling and creating more creative masterpieces. They will build on their previous working experience and on past marble run builds. Children will use their recall to rule out things that didn't work in the past. They will also use their memory to recall what worked in the past so they can replicate that success and build upon it.

This activity builds mental and physical abilities in a way that is fun and productive. Marble run success will have your children shouting for joy when it occurs, so be sure to see their completed work, and praise them for their efforts! **Hard work pays off and that is a lesson you want to teach when you praise them. It is the effort that matters most. This will help them take on greater challenges in the future because they will become more focused on the effort and not the outcome.**

95 Clothespin Letter Identification

Supplies Needed

☐ A piece of cardboard ☐ markers ☐ 27 clothespins

This is an inexpensive learning manipulative that you can create yourself with minimal time and effort. I used a piece of thin cardboard for this activity, which was a shirt insert used by our dry cleaners. We have a stack of these, and we get new cardboard sheets every time my husband has his shirts dry cleaned and folded. These pieces of cardboard are great for art projects, so don't throw them away if you get them from your dry cleaners or from new clothing you purchase.

First, I wrote the alphabet around the perimeter of the cardboard. I then wrote the alphabet out on clothespins. You will need 27 clothespins, one for each letter of the alphabet. Once you have this done it is ready for use!

Children use the clothespins as a matching exercise. They match the letter on their clothespin with the same letter on the cardboard. This activity helps them with letter identification, order of the alphabet, and helps develop their fine motor skills. Working with clothespins can take some practice for small children. Teach them how the clothespin works. They will develop hand and finger strength as they work with the clothespins for this activity.

96 Sheet Forts

☐ Sheets   ☐ blankets   ☐ chairs or a table

This activity was one we previously did with our couch cushions. That was lots of fun too, but I just got new furniture for our living room and didn't want the kids playing with our new cushions. We found it was quite easy and less effort to use some chairs to make a fort. This method allowed us to make a taller fort than the previous couch cushions created. We set up the chairs in a semi-circle and then draped them with a variety of blankets. We used three chairs. That way each of my three kids got their own space. They had the underside of their chair for them to stretch their legs out. This gave us plenty of space and thus no arguing. They used the tent to read, play, and do some coloring activities.

My kids begged to spend the night in it. That's up to you to decide for your own kids. We camp enough that I was able to say, no, but maybe another time. I simply didn't want my kids staying up too late and being crabby for Vacation Bible School the next morning. It is fun for them to camp out though. If you aren't a camping family, this is a great way to let them camp indoors and get that bonding time together. No need to buy a tent, just make your own fort using chairs, tables, and blankets or sheets. Provide them with some flashlights and tell a few stories by flashlight. It all goes a long way to creating an experience that will be full of great memories.

When children help to make a fort, they are using engineering and building skills. They are also learning how to plan things out and they get to figure out what works and doesn't work through trial and error. Don't set up the fort for them. Allow them to do most of the work if they are able. Every time they do something like this themselves, they are learning in the process. You are also helping them build their self-esteem and self-confidence.

97 Discover Kids Fort Construction Play

☐ A Construction Fort kit

We purchased this kit for our kids one Christmas. They spent the entire Christmas Day building with this kit! It was a favorite for all three of the kids that Christmas. This kit comes with construction rods and multifaceted connectors, which they use to make their own structures and forts. We got so much use out of the first set that we purchased a second one, so they could create even more elaborate structures. The two sets also helped keep arguing to a minimum since there were enough pieces for all three kids to create their own structures at the same time.

This activity is great for kids to work alone or together to create structures and designs. Some of these kits are labeled for five and up, but my twins started using them at age three under our supervision. They can be unsafe if children are poking one another with the construction sticks, so use your best judgment for your own children and supervise them while they are playing with this kit.

In playing with this kit, children are utilizing building and construction skills. They are also developing cognitive and problem-solving skills as they figure out what works and what doesn't. This is a creative and fun activity that gets them thinking and imagining all the things that they want to build. Then they get to work and try out their building skills and plans for themselves. It is a wonderful way for children to create their own designs, original thoughts, and plans in a way that is safe and fun. This activity also helps develop their spatial imagination.

When children collaborate to create structures with the fort construction kit they learn about teamwork. They will learn about cooperation and how to work successfully to execute a design plan. It is fun and educational at the same time!

98 Lacing Cards

Supplies Needed

☐ Lacing card kit

Lacing cards are typically sold in a kit with several cards and strings included. Since they are popular, you can find them at most stores with a toy section. They can also be purchased on Amazon, where you can find themed cards that your child may be more interested in playing with, such as dinosaurs or mermaids.

This activity is good for fine motor skill development. Children also improve their hand-eye coordination skills with this activity. It requires focus and concentration to do these projects, as the child must lace the string back and forth through the small holes on the card. However, children as young as age two can do this activity. It is so useful for fine motor skill development that is recommended by many occupational therapists.

You can make your own lacing cards. There are printables that can be found on Pinterest. Simply print the images on thicker paper, such as cardstock. You can also print on regular paper, cut out the image, and then trace it onto cardboard to be cut out. You can then use a hole punch to create the holes. A shoelace will work for the lacing. It can be an easy homemade activity if you are motivated to do it.

You can also make or buy lacing cards that are in the shapes of numbers and/or letters. Doing this lacing activity using these numbers and letters helps children with their number and letter recognition skills.

We have lots of lacing cards. They are used mostly on road trips. I have them in a gallon sized Ziploc, which makes it easy to take along in the car. Kids get their hands moving and they are learning while they play.

99 LEGO on the Go

- ☐ Art supply box
- ☐ LEGO bricks (or off brand blocks that work with LEGO products)
- ☐ cutting board
- ☐ glue that works on plastics
- ☐ a LEGO base plate.

This is one of three LEGO kits I created for my kids. Each of my children has one of these boxes, which we take with us on camping trips and road trips. We can't take our LEGO table with us, so these "LEGO on the Go" kits work wonderfully! This also makes cleanup a breeze, since everything gets put into one nice and neat container. I purchased the craft storage containers on sale at Michael's, and they came in a set of five. We have uses for the other containers, such as the one we use as a snack bin for road trips. Craft bins are so handy! They are sturdy too.

I purchased the blocks from the Dollar Tree. They also sell small base plates for $1. You can also purchase packages that contain 48 blocks for $1. I picked them up in a variety of colors and several base plates as well. They sold door and window kits for the blocks, which I also purchased for these kits. The nice thing about these blocks is that they work with LEGO products, as it states on their packing "fits all leading brands."

I purchased a small cutting board and glued down one of the base plates. This provides an easy to hold LEGO building space that can go in their lap (if in the car) or on a table or floor. I also picked up cups with suction cups on the bottom, which will be used on the cutting boards to hold blocks as they build in the car. This makes road trips more enjoyable for my twins, since they are obsessed with LEGO building. This way, they each get their own craft bin filled with these supplies for our summer travels and camping trips.

The cutting boards are also a useful idea for preschool or home use. You can purchase the larger 10" by 10" base plates on Amazon and then glue them onto larger cutting boards. The cutting boards are easy to store, don't take up much space, and then each child can have their own individual LEGO building space that can be moved from table, to floor, to desk with ease. Be sure to buy cutting boards that are not flexible. If they are flexible it will make it more difficult for the glue to hold the base plate. Use glue that is intended to bond plastics.

100 Recycling Center Play

Supplies Needed

☐ Three containers (we used foil tins) and items to sort for recycling

This idea is pretty simple. Take some foil containers and place a pile of items in the center. I wouldn't recommend using actual garbage. You can thoughtfully gather up safe metal, plastic, and paper items for this play activity. Then place one item in each container to get the ball rolling if your kids don't read yet, or you can tape a picture of the material to be recycled in the bottom of each of the trays. The recycling trucks pictured are from Walmart in case you want one for your home or classroom. This activity will help children with sorting skills, organizational thought processes, fine motor skill development, and learning through role play, as they pretend they're working at a recycling center. This is another easy activity that fosters learning and both cognitive and physical development.

Bonus One
101

Tag, Hide-n-Seek, and Chase

☐ Enough space for the children to play these games

Tag, hide-n-seek, and chase are games that have been around forever. They are all physical activities that get children moving and using their gross motor skills. These games are great because they don't require any planning or money. You only need some space for the children to play these games. Chase is the easiest, as children simply chase one another. It is like tag but can be done with only two children. One child chases the other and then they switch turns chasing. **Tag and chase are good old-fashioned playing that allows children to be children, while also developing their gross motor skills, social skills, and providing them with exercise.**

These are social games that get kids interacting through play. Children don't automatically know the rules for these games. They need to have someone tell them how these games work. Teach them the rules and keep it simple. Once they know how to play, let them play and have fun!

102

Playground Play

☐ A playground

Children love going to the playground. For many children this is by far their favorite place and activity. This is because children were made for physical play. They are naturally learning and developing through this type of physical play, which puts their gross motor skills into practice.

Vestibular stimulation is one of the greatest benefits of playground playtime. The vestibular system, discussed in Part I of this book, is the sensory system that enables our brain to develop spatial orientation, balance, motor function, and hand-eye coordination. A child's vestibular system is stimulated when they spin, slide, rock, and jump. These movements occur naturally while playing at a playground.

Since social interactions are a normal occurrence at a playground, playgrounds are also good for a child's socialization. Children learn to play cooperatively, to share playground equipment, and how to interact with others when they are playing at a playground. Playground time is also good for children emotionally, as they relax, play, and enjoy themselves on the equipment.

Children can benefit from playground playtime physically, emotionally, mentally, and socially. It is also a great way to keep children entertained for hours on end. One of the best investments we made for our children was the playset in our backyard. When we made the offer on our house, I asked our Realtor to include the backyard playground in the deal we were writing up. It was almost brand new. The couple had a corporate move, so they didn't know they were going to be moving shortly after investing in the playground. I was pregnant with our twins and our daughter was 18 months old. I knew we would be needing a backyard playset. I am glad they accepted our offer, and we got the playground with the house. It has been the most-used play item for all three of our kids. We forgot to ask that the kitchen refrigerator be included in our offer. They took that with them, even though it was a built-in version. Oh, well, at least we got the playset! The playground was obviously more important to me than a refrigerator. Our kids play for hours upon hours on our playset. **They only get to experience childhood once, so let them play!**

About the Author

Dr. Magdalena Battles has a PhD in psychology, a master's degree in professional counseling, and a bachelor of science degree in child psychology. Her post-graduate studies were completed at Harvard. She is a writer and conference speaker who specializes in parenting, child development, family relationships, domestic violence, and sexual assault. She shares her real-life experiences and professional insights on her website Living Joy Daily and on LifeHack.org, where she was named one of their top 10 writers. She and her family enjoy camping in the RV and have visited 26 national parks so far. Magdalena remains involved in her church and local community through Bible studies, book club, cheer coaching, and after-school programs. She and her husband reside in Texas where they are raising their three young children, a dog named Max, and a silkie chicken named Marshmallow. Magdalena is the author of *Let Them Play*.

http://livingjoydaily.com
https://www.facebook.com/groups/MomsEncouragingMoms1
https://www.facebook.com/groups/DrMagdalenaBattles

References

Battles, M. (2018). The endless battle between school work and play for children. Lifehack. https://www.lifehack.org/639509/the-endless-battle-between-school-works-and-play-for-children

Bongiorno, L. (2018). Talking with parents about play and learning. National Association for The Education of Young Children (NAEYC). https://www.naeyc.org/resources/pubs/tyc/aug2018/talking-parents-about-play-and-learning

Cohen, H., & Keshner, E.A. (1989). Current concepts of the vestibular system reviewed. *American Journal of Occupational Therapy*, 43, 331-338. https://ajot.aota.org/article.aspx?articleid=1880102

Duckworth, A. (2018). *Grit*. New York, NY: Scribner.

Eckart, K. (2017). How reading and writing with your child boost more than just literacy. University of Washington. http://www.washington.edu/news/2017/08/28/how-reading-and-writing-with-your-child-boost-more-than-just-literacy

Gillbert, R. (2017). Science says parents of successful kids have 17 things in common. Business Insider. https://www.businessinsider.com/how-to-raise-successful-kids-2017-3

Goodwin, G. (2018). To play is to learn. Time to step back and let kids be kids. World Economic Forum. https://www.weforum.org/agenda/2018/01/to-play-is-to-learn

Integrated Learning Strategies (2016). Vestibular system: Bring back playground equipment with a little danger. Integrated Learning Strategies Learning Corner. https://ilslearningcorner.com/2016-01-vestibular-system-bring-back-playground-equipment-with-a-little-danger

Martin (2017). 11 ways to raise successful kids. Healthy Way. https://www.healthyway.com/content/ways-to-raise-successful-kids

National Association for The Education of Young Children (2018). NAEYC early learning program accreditation standards and assessment items. NAEYC. https://www.naeyc.org/sites/default/files/globallyshared/downloads/PDFs/accreditation/early-learning/standards_and_assessment_web_1.pdf#page=39

National Association for the Education of Young Children (2009). Developmentally appropriate practice in early childhood programs serving children from birth through age 8: A position statement of the National Association for the Education of Young Children. NAEYC. https://www.naeyc.org/sites/default/files/globally-shared/downloads/PDFs/resources/position-statements/PSDAP.pdf

Rettner, R. (2011). Are today's youth less creative & imaginative? Live Science. https://www.livescience.com/15535-children-creative.html

Schoning & Witcomb (2017). This is the one skill your child needs for jobs of the future. World Economic Forum. https://www.weforum.org/agenda/2017/09/skills-children-need-work-future-play-lego

Suggate, Schaughency, and Reese (2013). Children learning to read later catch up to children reading earlier. *The Early Childhood Research Quarterly*, vol 28(1), Issue 1. https://www.sciencedirect.com/science/article/pii/S0885200612000397#!

Wojcicki, E. (2019). I raised two CEOs and a doctor. These are my secrets to parenting successful children. *TIME*. https://time.com/5578064/esther-wojcicki-raise-successful-kids

Made in the USA
Monee, IL
06 September 2020